What is Magic?

Volume I of the Introduction to Magic series

Bob Makransky

Copyright © 2012, 2014 by Bob Makransky

ISBN-13: 978-0967731568

Published by Dear Brutus Press

http://www.amzn.com/1499279418

Table of Contents

The Magician's Creed …………..	2
Acknowledgements ……………...	4
Foreword by Michael Peter Langevin	5
1 – Introduction ………………..	14
2 – Spirits ………………………	24
3 – Intent ………………………	33
4 – The Nature of Reality ……...	42
5 – Spells, Charms, and Rituals ..	50
6 – Science Debunked …………	64
7 – Demons ……………………	80
8 – The Nature of the Self ……...	92
9 – Bewitching …………………	102
10 – Magic and Money ………...	112
11 – Death ……………………..	121
12 – Black Magicians & Vampires	128
13 – Power Places ……………...	141
14 – The Magician's God ……...	147
15 – Magical Time ……………..	152
16 – Magic and Morality ………	157
17 – Dreaming and Stalking …...	163
18 – Magic and Sex ……………	175
19 – Bibliography of Magic …….	185
Glossary ………………………..	193
Books by Bob Makransky …………	195

The Magician's Creed

*You are the people,
You are this season's people –
There are no other people this season.
If you blow it, it's blown.*
– Stephen Gaskin

I. The human race is in imminent danger of self-destructing and dragging our mother earth down with it.

II. There will be no miraculous salvation due to Mayan prophecies; or Jesus' or the Mahdi's return; much less from the irresponsible governments, corporations, media, and academics who got us into this mess in the first place.

III. The theory of probable realities states that each individual person decides the fate of the entire universe. If you truly choose to save the world, you will wind up in a probable reality in which the world is saved.

IV. The only chance for survival – not to mention prosperity – is for each individual to reject society's mutual suicide pact and make saving the earth and future generations their NUMBER 1 PRIORITY (as opposed to something they may get around to someday). This is the magician's equivalent of the Bodhisattva's oath.

V. Rejecting social conditioning means eradicating all trace of self-pity. Only by clear, sober, objective thinking (not unquestioning adherence to beliefs) can each individual save him/herself and the earth.

VI. This type of thinking is based upon what each person's heart tells them. It is different for everybody; and everybody has to find their own answers for themselves by examining their own habitual thoughts, moods, and concerns minutely. To do this magicians use various techniques, including:
    a) techniques of self-analysis such as Active Imagination and Recapitulation.
    b) techniques of transformation such as resorting to tree spirits and the earth.
    c) techniques of hopefulness such as Creative Visualization.

VII. Detaching from society's conditioning of self-pity necessarily implies taking complete responsibility for oneself rather than wallowing in helplessness or daydreaming. To do this magicians:
    a) channel their own spirit guides themselves for information and advice;
    b) go to nature spirits for validation rather than seek the approval of other people or society;
    c) become as self-sufficient and frugal as possible, including growing at least some of their own food and reducing their needs to the bare minimum.

VIII. The goal of magic is to make everyday life more dreamlike; to be able to feel comfortable in situations beyond one's control. Feeling relaxed and in good shape even in the midst of a maelstrom is called "enlightenment". Enlightenment doesn't mean light as opposed to dark; but rather light as opposed to heavy.

Acknowledgements

The author would like to thank Milly Mittelstaedt, Diane Simpo Lambrinos, and Bob Wachtel for their many helpful suggestions. I am especially grateful to Robert Mattis for his yeomanly work in editing the original manuscript. Many of these essays originally appeared in *Diamond Fire* magazine, and thanks are due to Joseph Polansky for permission to publish them here. Thanks are also due to Juan Carlos Lemus for permission to reproduce his photograph of the sacred Mayan grotto of Chicoy (*Mojcuan* – km 169 north of Purulha, B.V.) on the cover. The Chapter "Science Debunked" Copyright © 2009 *Dell Horoscope Magazine*. Reprinted with permission. Special thanks to Ronnie Grishman for this use.

Author's note: this book was originally written in 2005-2006; some of the references in the text (to e.g. Fukushima, and the economic crisis of 2008) were added later.

What is Magic?

Foreword

by Michael Peter Langevin

Publisher, *Magical Blend* magazine

When Bob asked me to write the introduction to this book, I was a bit apprehensive. However, when I read over his manuscript, I was thrilled and honored. Bob is daring, willing to be offensive with his truths, and wise in the ways of words and magic. The question of what I could add to such a great piece haunted me. I finally decided that I would discuss my personal experiences, for I have believed in, experienced, and practiced magic all my life. I have been living as magically as possible for decades.

I know this period in which we now dwell is unique to humanity's, Earth's, and the entire universe's existence. Books and information comparable to what Bob reveals in this great book are essential to bringing about the best possible outcomes for all. From birth, humans are told in countless ways that they are stupid, not good enough, powerless victims, and that their creative expressions are weak and useless. They are often given the impression that the world is very limited and they will not be likely to get their needs met, much less achieve their dreams. But that way of viewing the world and how we should live is flawed. It robs life of its meaning and negates the ability for anyone to matter. Rather, we all need to learn to trust more, relax more, laugh more, demand prosperity, wealth, power, fame, joy, fulfillment, and even ecstasy. We need to test the limits of our creative expressions and of every aspect of ourselves. However, being driven, overworked, over-achievers is not the way we must learn to accomplish this, but through magic flowing with the energies of our world. When we pray, we ask the Gods for what we want. When we meditate, we listen to what the Gods want. When we create, we become one with the Gods. When we perform, and refine, and even live magic, we surpass the Gods.

All religions tell of miracles. Moses brought forth water in the desert; Jesus healed the sick, raised the dead, multiplied the bread and fish to feed the hungry, changed water into wine, and even walked on water. Mohammed heard God's words and wrote them down. Buddha attained Nirvana. Krishna ended wars. They were all Magic workers and examples of what any human can achieve. None were the one-and-only path; none possessed the one-and-only truth. Any who proclaim that these teachers had all the answers are ignorant, power-hungry, deluded or evil. And neither does magic offer or claim that it is the one true path. Every book, teacher, religion or culture contains good and bad information and tools. Magicians must choose what feels right for them at every point in their lives. Magic, when researched, refined, and practiced works and creates miracles.

In this book, Bob explores magic, sex, and love. In a committed relationship, you learn about yourself, and to make it last you must become better at compromise, and be willing to see your mate as a mirror of the lessons you need to learn and of weaknesses you otherwise refuse to see in yourself. Children give you the opportunity to learn about tolerance, trust and many elements of your being that exist in your subconscious that were either embedded there from past lives or the first ten to twenty years of your life.

The wealthiest and most controlling corporations, who fight for power and feed on human suffering, use sex to sell useless products and then tell humans in every other way that free, open sexual experiences are evil, wrong unfulfilling, unhealthy, and sinful. Many humans live in guilt, shame, or denial. Even many who become Tantric teachers and Sorcerers, skilled in sacred sexual secrets, seldom can escape all of society's negative messages.

In the bygone days of pre-western, pre-organized religion; most people, especially shamans and high priestesses, viewed sex as one of the easiest and most powerful ways to perform magic and increase one's personal, spiritual evolution. The Inca of Peru, and many African and Latin American pre-Conquest peoples, knew magical sexual techniques that produced such exceedingly powerful and ecstatic states that we could scarcely imagine today. I have met Incan magicians in isolated Andean villages who have brought me to sexual states beyond most peoples' dreams. These sexual techniques can be researched and recreated by imaginative, magical lovers.

By sharing open sex, lust, and maybe even romance with new and different lovers you can learn about seduction, telepathy, and intuition. You share in the fulfillment of physical joy, and when it's great, you share ecstasy. When magic is effectively incorporated, the two of you melt into a single synergetic puddle of pure, indefinable desires and hopes surpassed. Such lovers become one with the Divine essence of all that is, the force that created this very universe. Pure, shared, lustful sex, which must be both selfish and selfless at once, is one of the most potent kinds of magic that humans can perform. But be warned; it is like fire, and it can warm you up to new states of existence or burn you if poorly used.

Magic and Death

In the past two years, my father, my mother, and my second grade teacher, who was a member of the Theosophical Society since 1949 and my friend and mentor for fifty years, all left their physical bodies. They were perhaps the three who most cared and knew about more of my life and achievements than any others, and they all departed from my life on this physical plane within a twenty-four month period. I felt abandoned and depressed. I knew their souls still existed and would continue on forever. However, I could not call, write, visit them, or verbally receive their wisdom, feedback, or guidance.

I have been able to astral travel since age 13. It usually required a week of fasting, meditation, and ritual. To achieve it in dreams, it often demanded great amounts of self-hypnosis and focus for days or weeks. I read and re-read many astral traveling and lucid dreaming books. I also read many books, which explored life after death in a nonreligious way. Then, I took a week-long class from the Monroe Institute on mastering altered states and astral travel. Now, weekly in my dreams, I am able to visit with my three dead advisors, separately in different astral places, and they share spiritual insights and magic with me.

I teach my children that their lives should be dedicated to exploring how the world works and then developing ways to make it serve them and those they care about. I tell them that it is indeed possible to achieve their goals and desires. This is the essence of magic to me. I view earth and humanity as a sea of potential. I see them as seedpods ready to burst and spread their fertile seeds into the winds to travel, fall, and grow in a myriad of ways. Presently, we live in a material world limited by our five senses and controlled by media and wealthy power brokers. However, there are in truth no limits to what any one person can become, create, or achieve. The only limits are our personal imagination, beliefs, desires, motivations, and dedication.

Many people must believe I'm crazy or delusional! After all, I hear voices, speak with Gods, Goddesses, dead friends and relatives, angels, demons, and a hoard of other invisible beings. Yet, I have created from nothing an international magazine company, and I have been the CEO and President of that prosperous business for over 25 years. I have been more happily than not married for over 22 years, and I have successfully raised two well-adjusted children who get good grades in school, are great athletes, great writers and campers, and who like themselves and have many good friends. I have also written three books, which have sold very well. To me, these are all manifestations of the effective use of Magic.

Creation and Rebirth through Magic

Reality is not our material world as perceived by our five senses. Our day-to-day reality, where we exist in this life, is only a small, unimportant aspect of reality. Reality is limitless and largely unperceivable by our normal senses. When a person reads this wonderful book that explores magic, he or she will either not believe it, be frightened by it, think it's too time consuming and too life altering; or it will illuminate an important aspect of their sleeping self. If it does awaken you, then the challenges begin. Magic is seldom easy! It demands risk-taking, persistence, and a willingness to make major mistakes and to dance with insanity itself. Not only is magic real, it is one of the few choices people have which will lead them to their unimagined potential. All humans are potentially limitless divine beings. We each can, in a matter of ten or twenty years, learn to not only perceive and visit fantastic otherworldly dimensions but to use magic to create the lives we want, the world we want, and even the reality we want. If we are not pleased, or become bored, we can create countless other lives, worlds, and realities, where no one controls us but ourselves. Magic is limitless. You can start small by building up successes, skills, experiences, allies, and miracles, yet always set your life goals beyond your imagination and live towards achieving all you can.

    I have a magician friend who is tied into the Monroe institute and, like myself, has read a million spiritual books. He is so connected with many of his past lives and has such bad health that he doesn't want to be in his current life anymore. In his youth, he used his magic to achieve wealth and many amazing accomplishments, but now he has come to strongly believe that there are many alternative earths and that on many he is still very ambitious and goal-oriented. However, on this one, he now just wants to play at practicing his magic and doing some healings. He feels that my constant drive, intensity, passion, and ambition are exhausting and unnecessary. He says I need to trust in the universe more, that everything is fine as it is, and that we aren't meant to nor able to save anything or anyone, or build anything unique. I say and believe strongly that he is wrong. We argue over this often. I believe we were created to experience joy, love, ecstasy, and many other things as only we can; each of us has a life mission, and we can achieve it and beyond, but many get lost and fail to accomplish their ultimate goals. Each individual has a spark of greatness and the potential to create a life and things in ways no one else ever could or will be able to again. I believe we all have a responsibility to do our best to magically create, experience, and enhance every aspect of existence. Arguing with this friend forces me to reaffirm that the contradictory statement I have always said is true: nothing matters, yet everything is important.

I have recently read another new author who believes that Earth and Humans are a dying shade world, which was created with the potential to create countless fantastic high-energy worlds and alternative dimensions, but, like the dinosaurs and many other experimental races with unique potential, it failed. She asserts that in her view only a few powerful, high-energy, well-disciplined individuals will break out of the entropy and become creator Gods. I believe it isn't over yet. I am unsure if this is the only Earth or if there is one for every decision that every person makes, or if there is something in-between. However, I believe we have a responsibility to live as if this is the only chance and that every one of our thoughts, words, and deeds make a major difference. In the comic books there is a superhero. He is a human with God-like, nearly limitless super powers, far beyond Superman's capabilities. He invented a computer, which monitors all world events and weighs the priorities to help him decide where and for whom to save the day so that his actions do the most good by his value system. I think we all should live that way. We should first become clear on our values and goals and realize that they are always changing and hopefully evolving. Then, we must devise short term goals and action plans to achieve our life's mission. Self-evolution, self awareness and healing, and honesty to ourselves must always be high priorities, followed closely by helping other humans, the planet, and nature. Furthermore, we must feel free to create in whatever ways we are most inspired. For me, creation mostly comes in the forms of writing, teaching and lecturing, and exploring how to better spread empowering, inspiring information.

To accomplish our mission, we must develop somewhat healthy and balanced lives. We all require time to rest, time to laugh, time to read, time to exercise, and times to cultivate and maintain our closest relationships. Anyone we get close to can and, usually does, serve as a mirror, showing us our weaknesses and areas in which we need to grow. I feel that my magical, unmotivated friend is running from and avoiding some major lessons; therefore, he will not become all he can be in this life. None of us are perfect; however, we must strive

What is Magic?

for the best. We must forgive others and ourselves for our weaknesses and mistakes. With open hearts, we must passionately live every moment to its fullest. My life has not measured up to my ultimate goal or vision yet. However, if I died today, at least I will have spent most of my years living and savoring all I was given as best I could.

What do readers need to know before devouring this great book of magic? Most importantly, you need to imagine that you might be reading this book because it is time for you to awaken to the next stage of your growth and evolution. When a brilliant, intellectual, worldly friend of mine first was exposed to magic as a reality, she said it felt like she had been given a totally new world view, comparable to starting over in kindergarten.

Demons, Magic, and Religious Teachings

Over 1000 years ago many people lived in ignorance and many more lived with knowledge that today's people have little awareness of. Before organized religion, people everywhere knew and used magic and ritual. Religions came into existence to keep society hopeful and provide spiritual reminders. However, more so, there are those of us who believe that religions also came into power to control the masses, keep humanity at war over their opposing beliefs, destroy and hide magical knowledge and empowering information, and concentrate focus on after life rewards. The inquisitions happen differently in Asia and India, but they do happen. In order for an organized twentieth-century religion to grow and maintain followers, it must teach that it has the only real truths and that only its leaders can talk to the God or Gods, or know the real paths to Nirvana. They must preach that all other beliefs are wrong. They all have closed minds and hearts. Some of the most cruel, hateful people I have ever known were devotedly religious, yet some of the most spiritually open people were also religious. The first were vengeful leaders and blind, weak followers. The second group was comprised of open-minded, open-hearted missionaries who were forgiving and loving.

Multitudes of powerful, spiritual beings exist in the astral planes. Many, at one point in history, have been worshipped as Gods. There are also evil and powerful negative forces that exist and influence humanity. I personally went through a brief period in my life when I was selfish and extremely insecure. I believed that only the dark side could give me power and manifest my dreams. I was effective in persuading demons to do what I asked of them and to give me results at others' expense. I didn't even try to care. In no time at all, the demons took over, undid all they had done, and began ruining all aspects of my life. I suffered from nightmares and near insanity until, finally, I prayed to Jesus, Mary, Mohammed, Buddha, Krishna, and Gaia for help and forgiveness. They banished the demons, and I was free to rebuild a healthy life based on positive, loving magic dedicated to helping, uplifting, and empowering all whom I met or influenced. Once, after that experience, I met LaVey, the author of *The Satanic Bible* and the founder of the church of Satan. He was powerful, rich, and had beautiful young girls waiting on him. He had effectively made a deal with the dark side all his life. He was a great success, but now he is dead. I have seen his spirit suffering and know it will for ages. We all make choices.

Emotions are a challenge to control, especially jealousy, hate, insecurity, loneliness, and rage; but a magician must learn control. Anger can be a good source of power if focused towards ending a bad situation or achieving better results, but as with jealousy and hate, it is only effective when refocused. Love, desire, unselfish lust, honor, ambition, and pride of achievement are all what powerful magic uses. In truth, the most spiritually evolved people I have encountered have moved beyond letting anything affect them in the least. They have an inner balance and trust that allows them to deal with winning the lottery and the death of a lover in the same manner. One day I hope to achieve such detachment; today I am still an over-achiever with many mood swings.

Is my life, or that of any powerful, wise magic worker, perfect and free from worries, setbacks, failures, disappointments, major mistakes or temptations? Not on this earth. At every step that any dedicated magic worker takes, new challenges arise. There are often setbacks and temptations to succumb to actions and life styles that are negative for you and those you interact with. I meet many spiritual people who one year seem nearly enlightened and wise far beyond me. When I often encounter them again years later, they have become disenchanted or discouraged. Many have fallen into drug addiction, alcoholism, sexual exploitation of students, or even suicide. The temptations and challenges never stop in this life. However, a magician knows that we can always undo our mistakes and get back to where we were if we allow ourselves to reawaken, but in every life on earth there are always challenges and failures that provide us with the opportunity to learn, grow, and evolve our lives and our magic.

Bob Makransky, I feel, has written a great treatise on magic. I urge you to enjoy it as much as I have.

Yours in Spirit,

Michael Peter Langevin

I – Introduction

The purpose of this book is to show you that magic really works. Without radically altering your present lifestyle you can step into a world of magic and wonder.

Magic is simply a matter of tuning out the constant static of society and the babble of other people, and listening to your own heart. You don't need a guru, or a therapist, or anyone to tell you how to listen to your heart. All you have to do is remember the original knowledge you were born with, which has been distorted by the influence of your environment (conditioning by your parents and society). This book will help you to do that. This book will help you hear your heart's message. That's why you found it.

Magic is a point of view, a slant on everyday life. The magical point of view, however, is very different from present-day society's point of view that e.g. spirits don't exist. They do, however. You know this in your heart. You have had psychic, paranormal experiences yourself – otherwise, you wouldn't be reading this book.

Magic is not a matter of altered states of consciousness, or of ooga-booga rituals (although it does involve such things). Rather, it's a matter of taking a good, hard look at your present situation. Magic means examining your everyday life and yourself objectively. Magic requires seeing yourself with no personal feelings at all, as if you were a detached critic. Rather than believing what society says (and has trained you to believe) that magic is an escape from reality, in fact the practice of magic entails directly coming to grips with reality.

Magic is as ancient as humankind, but it has been forgotten in all the rush to make a buck and to fulfill other people's expectations. Now the time for magic has come around again. Magic and astrology will rise once more if the human race is to survive, not to mention prosper.

These are heady times. We can all feel the change in the air, the crackle of energy. We sense that human consciousness is going through a fundamental transformation. The human race is coming to a crunch. Human society and human

What is Magic?

consciousness are on the brink of a major breakthrough; or else of self-destruction. More and more people are casting about looking for straight answers that they're not getting from their governments, media, academics, or churches. Luckily all the answers and tools you need are right there, in your own heart, if you could only connect to it. The practice of magic will help you to make that connection.

Magic can be defined as *the intentional manipulation of luck by means of the deliberate cultivation of intuition*. Most people believe that luck and intuition are haphazard affairs. Magicians, however, seek to control them.

Is magic real? It most certainly is, but not in the sense in which the popular media, such as the American television program *Charmed*, would have you believe. On television and in movies magicians are portrayed as having special powers that they are born with, such as freezing or repelling enemies, making things appear and disappear, and so forth. This is untrue (although the scene in which Kim Novak bewitched Jimmy Stewart in the movie *Bell, Book, and Candle* is actually not that far off the mark). Magicians are like everyone else, but perhaps are more psychic and intuitive than the norm. The difference between magicians and most people is one of degree rather than of kind.

Magicians tend to be more rebellious than average, and less fearful of the consequences of their rebellion. Ever since childhood they've known that they were different somehow, that they didn't fit in; and most likely they were castigated for this by their family and schoolmates. Magicians tend not to trust in what they were taught – in what everyone around them is taking for granted – and they tend to be more ready to fly with their impulses than are average people.

This misperception about magic and magicians is a shame, since the truth about magic is far more interesting, compelling, and personally applicable in your own life than the false stereotypes which appear in the popular media.

It's not that magicians have supernormal powers. Rather, from the magicians' point of view, most people are walking around with both hands – their intuition and intent – tied behind their backs. They are paralyzed by their fear of disapproval; by their fear of death; by their fear of life. They learn this fear from their parents and society, and they pass it on to their own children in turn.

Thus, to most people, magicians' use of their "hands" seems like the use of supernormal powers. However, magicians have no power beyond what most people possess – they just use their power. They use their intuition to process incoming information, and they use their intent to influence the outside world.

Most magicians don't even know that they are magicians. They do not understand or consider what they are doing to be magic, since it comes so naturally to them. Magicians who happen to be Christians or capitalists would scoff at the idea that they are magicians using magic. But anyone who applies the techniques of magic to get what they want from life, anyone who has some degree of mastery in the use of intuition and intent, is a magician.

A story about General George Patton provides an example of the magician in all of us. In the middle of the night on Christmas Eve during the Battle of the Bulge in December 1944, General Patton jumped out of his bed and called his secretary in to take an order. During his sleep he had intuited that the Germans would mount an attack at a certain spot the next day. In anticipation of this move, Patton decided to mount an attack of his own to preempt the German offensive. When Christmas day dawned Patton's counterattack hit the Germans just as they began and stopped them cold, thus averting what could have been a serious threat to Patton's flank. A few days later, commenting on this episode, Patton told his secretary: "To tell you the truth, I didn't know at all that the German attack was coming. In the future some people will call it luck and some will call it genius."

"What would you call it, General?" his secretary asked. Patton paused and then replied, "Determination."[1]

What Patton termed "determination" is what we refer to in this book as "intent." Intent is the driving force behind magic.

Actually, we are all magicians. We are all performing magic all the time. Just to exist in this world requires

What is Magic?

considerable magical ability and prowess. Anybody who is highly successful and original, such as Bill Gates, for example, is using the principles of magic unknowingly. The appellation "magician" in fact transcends species. Magicians are born amongst all species: there are hawk magicians, whale magicians, oak magicians, and so forth. Magicians of any species are recognizable since they are basically outsiders who go their own way and prefer solitude to the company of other members of their species.

Human magicians actually have more in common with animal or plant magicians than they do with other humans who are not magicians. What magicians pay attention to and seek in everyday life is quite different from what most people pay attention to and seek. Most people seek security and comfort. Magicians seek freedom. The two goals are incompatible.

Most people believe that they and the world surrounding them are real. Magicians believe that the world and the self are merely projections, like a movie on a screen or the shadows in Plato's cave.

Where most people seek to manipulate the world for their advantage and convenience, magicians seek to manipulate their perception. That is to say, magicians change the world by changing their perception of it, rather than by fussing about trying to make things happen outside themselves.

Where most people are guided by the conventional thinking of their culture and epoch, magicians, both black and white, are guided by spirits until they get their own intuition and intent working.

Unlike the Abrahamic religions (which include rationalistic materialism – the pseudo-science practiced in academia), magic is not a belief system – it is a cognitive system. It is a way of apprehending rather than thinking; it is a way of acting rather than talking. Magicians draw anything they need directly from the Spirit rather than from what other people have told them or might think of them.

Average people always seem to be looking for a free ride or escape from their problems. They hope and believe that they will someday have an epiphany; or meet a true guru or a soul-mate; or win the lottery; and from then on all their problems will be solved. However, even people who have had epiphanies, or met true gurus or soul-mates, or won the lottery, found that this didn't particularly solve anything for them. Do you believe that the rich and famous are any happier than anyone else?

Hoping for some fantasy to come true in order to be happy is absurd. It's like believing in Santa Claus. Life just isn't like that, except in the movies, and magicians are supreme realists. Most of what magicians do isn't done by supernormal means, but by facing squarely the way things really are, and accepting the situation in which they find themselves right now.

The secret of magic, which is commonly misunderstood, is to adapt to circumstances rather than try to dominate or control circumstances. It's by adapting yourself as best you can without losing your hope and intent, without letting your circumstances crush you or surrendering to your self-pity, that you can change your circumstances.

The first step in magic is to get beyond your assumptions. This means seeing them clearly in the first place. It implies seeing yourself as others do, for starters.

Magicians don't take anything for granted. They have no specific expectations, and the only assumption they make is that whatever happens will be a big surprise. Isn't it usually the case that when the solutions to your problems finally do come, they scarcely ever happen the way you anticipated and fantasized that they would?

Thus, magicians don't have to think as much as most people do. They don't have to worry, or plan, or scheme about the future. Nor do magicians hide their shame from the past. They don't care as much as most people do about what has happened or what will happen; or what anybody thinks about them. They know they have no real control over either their past or future, so they don't have to defend what they did or worry about what they might do.

The terms "magic" and "shamanism" or "witchcraft" are interchangeable. The main difference between paganism and magic is that paganism is a religion and magic is a technology.

What is Magic?

However the two are closely entwined for many practitioners, although you can be a magician without being a pagan. Indeed, in the literal sense of the word, there are Christian magicians, Buddhist magicians, Hindu magicians, scientist magicians, banker magicians, star athlete magicians, and so on. Anyone who is using magic to further their intent, whether they are conscious of what they are doing or not, has to be considered a magician. Thus while many pagans are also magicians, not all magicians are also pagans.

Magic can be considered a spiritual path. It is a path in which you are given a lot more power than you have earned. In trying to control this power you are forced to put the rest of your life in order. Thus power is the spur and motivation to action.

What is power, then? It can be considered the same thing as luck, freedom, or responsibility. Power and freedom are the same thing. They both arise upon taking complete responsibility for your own destiny instead of just drifting along, hoping something will fall at your feet.

What is responsibility? It is not blaming other people, or God, for your own unhappiness. Rather, it is understanding that you have deliberately, if unconsciously, chosen the situations in which you find yourself.

For us as individuals to try to reconstruct magic in this dark age of materialism is tantamount to an intellectual adventurer a thousand years from now who stumbles upon some relic PC's and, knowing of legends that the ancients had machines which could think, sets out to reconstruct computer knowledge by himself.

Magic, like computer science, is most effective if society as a whole is devoting much of its energy to it. One or a few scattered individuals working alone can't accomplish much; however it is a start. Magic is an ancient knowledge which it is now our duty as a society to reconstruct if the human race is to survive, not to mention progress.

FAQ's

Does magic really exist? The answer is yes. It most assuredly does exist. The problem is that existence doesn't exist. Another way of saying this is, "You create your own reality." For example, the realities of children and primitive peoples are indeed magical, so for them magic exists. They can see it at work all the time. However our modern lifestyle trains you to reject your intuition and inner feelings about the nature of your world. By the time most people reach adulthood they have shut down their intuitive channels and rejected the belief that they have power over their world.

Do magicians have supernatural power? This depends upon your definition of "supernatural." Magicians do have supernatural power, but so does everybody else. Magicians have just consciously developed their power through training.

What is "power"? It's the same thing as luck. Luck is actually a better word for it, but the term "luck" as commonly used connotes something outside of your conscious control. You think of power as something you can consciously command. In fact, this isn't really true: it is power which commands you. But at least magicians are consciously aware of what's happening. Luck, on the other hand, seems serendipitous because you don't see the connection – how you are making your own luck.

What about powers like psychic healing, seeing auras, crystal gazing, knowing the future, communicating with spirits, astral projection, etc.? These are all abilities which can be developed with practice. Some people have such gifts from birth due to their karma from past lives and their particular purpose for incarnating in this lifetime.

What about stopping one's enemies with a psychic blast, or making things appear or disappear, or bewitching people? For the most part the powers that magicians have on television or in the movies are fantasy. One thing that is factually correct about how magicians with special powers are portrayed in the popular media is that having special powers isn't much help in dealing with everyday life. Bewitching

What is Magic?

other people is possible. Everybody is doing it to everyone else, albeit subconsciously, already. This will be explained later on.

Do vampires really exist? Yes, we'll talk about that later too. Suffice it to say that what vampires do is only an extreme form of something most people are doing to each other all the time anyway, namely sucking other people's energy.

I've tried using spells I've gotten out of books, but they don't work. This is because other people's spells are pretty much useless. It's your own intent that matters, not the words you say. To make spells work you have to have faith. It's the certainty that a spell will work which makes it work.

Do we really create our own realities? Much of the time it would seem that this isn't true. It appears that things "just happen". But what about your dreams? Do you create them, or do they just happen?

Earlier it was said that existence doesn't exist. What this means is that what you experience when you are awake is just a dream. This is literally true. It certainly seems that what you experience in the everyday world, while you are awake, is "real". However the dreams you had last night certainly seemed real also at the time you were dreaming them.

Similarly, it is merely your belief that what happens to you while you are awake is real, that makes it real. Just as when you awaken from a dream you realize that it wasn't real, so too is there a point of view from which you can awaken from being awake and realize that being awake isn't real either. That point of view is magic.

Most people intuit that magic *is* real, that it *does* work, because they can still remember from childhood that the world is magical. Usually this memory is unconscious. On a conscious level you probably have forgotten what you knew as a child: that the world is basically a happy place; that the sun and wind and clouds and rain are alive, and can talk to you and tell you their secrets.

Unfortunately for the seeker after truth, there is lots of misinformation floating around. New Age writers are often no more truthful than are scientists and academics. This is because lots of people who are ostensibly into magic don't really want true information. For them it's just an image they have of themselves, but they're actually afraid of true knowledge, as well they should be. To be a true magician requires tremendous courage and willingness to follow one's own intuition and intent, no matter what society or other people think. Don't believe for a minute that anyone is going to strew your path with rose petals – quite the contrary!

Being a magician necessitates uncompromising honesty with yourself. It entails, for example, facing the fact of your death directly, every day in every way. It entails seeing yourself clearly, with all your flaws and selfishness. It entails giving up the belief that you're special: that anyone, including God, owes you anything or will help or save you. It entails understanding that you aren't going to suddenly have your luck change without you taking 100% responsibility yourself for making your dreams come true.

The reason why many people are afraid of magic isn't because they're afraid it is evil, which is what churches and sensationalist media have told them. Rather, it is because they are afraid of taking 100% responsibility for and control over their own lives. It is much easier to believe in fables like "You will go to heaven when you die" or "Your investments will still be solvent when you're ready to retire" or "Three Mile Island and Chernobyl were flukes – that'll never happen again." (this was written before Fukushima). It's easier to fall under the spell of the lullabies which society sings to you to keep you from thinking for yourself, than to face up to the truth.

The truth is that there isn't any security in life. Neither God nor society care about what happens to you. You have no one and nothing to rely upon except yourself.

Magicians train themselves to take full responsibility for their lives. This gives them confidence in dealing with whatever may come, be it illness, poverty, death, or whatever else may happen. This is the basic tenet of magic. It is a truth that many people are afraid to face because they don't understand that being vulnerable and defenseless does not necessarily mean being helpless and powerless. On the contrary, it's the doorway to freedom.

Notes:

[1] Farago, Ladislas, *Patton: Ordeal and Triumph*, Dell NYC 1963 page 254.

II – Spirits

Most people rely upon the dictates of their society to know what to do – what they've been taught by their parents, teachers, pastors, bosses, advertisers, and the media. Magicians, by contrast, rely upon the counsel of spirits, at least until they've got their own intuition and intent operating.

In truth, I don't know what spirits are; and this is said after twenty-five years of intimate acquaintance with them.[1] The problem is that as humans we tend to impose features of the known upon the unknown. We want to make the unknown familiar and comfortable to deal with, so we naturally tend to regard spirits in terms which are already familiar to us – we can't be wholly objective about them. What I will describe here is my own view of what spirits are, based upon my own interactions with them.

My materialist friends, who reject the existence of spirits, do usually credit my integrity. They don't question my belief that spirits are communicating with me, but they think that I'm mistaken in my interpretation that the spirits are outside of me rather than parts of my own psyche. However, I do make a distinction between my own thought forms such as inner child, lower self, anima and animus on the one hand, and spirits on the other.

I really don't know what spirits are, or whether they are inside or outside of us. I do know that every religion and culture in the world except materialistic science is based upon spirit communication.

Christians, for example, often forget that their religion is spiritualistic. Jesus is a spirit; the Virgin Mary is a spirit; and of course the Holy Spirit, needless to say, is a spirit. When Christians say: "Jesus talks to me and guides me," that's what magicians call channeling. Christians and magicians use different spirits, but the technical basis – communication between spirits and people – is the same in all religions.

Have you ever noticed how rituals in many different religions have basically the same accoutrements? They all tend to take place in darkened rooms with candles and incense

What is Magic?

smoke, with monotonous chanting or litanies repeated over and over. The reason for this is because spirits themselves like such things: darkness, smoke, repetitive incantations. Originally, and still today in traditional religions, the purpose of religious ritual was to make contact with the spirit world. Participants enter a light trance state to make them more accessible to spirit messages. Religious rituals originally were magical acts. In the Roman Catholic mass, for example, bread and wine are magically transformed into the body and blood of Jesus.

Recent converts to any religion often experience a high, a state of grace, which usually doesn't last very long. These epiphanies are gifts of spirits who have the capacity to temporarily lower people's sense of self-importance and self-pity, which in turn opens their hearts. This often happens when people are at the end of their rope with nowhere to turn. It's often at such times of complete desperation that they open to the Spirit and allow grace to descend upon them. This state of grace is channeled through spirit intermediaries such as Jesus, Krishna, or Buddha. This grace is usually temporary because the people still have inner work to do in order to embody the state of grace permanently in their everyday lives.

Spirits can temporarily bestow grace on people who are open to it – usually because they've exhausted their own resources. But it's not the spirits' job to carry emotional cripples on their backs forever. Spirits can reveal a temporary glimpse of open-heartedness to animate people to seek such spiritual goals on their own. Having been given a model of what to strive for, it becomes the responsibility of the individual to continue the work begun by the spirits.

Everyone is receiving messages from spirits, both angelic and demonic ones, all the time. However in our society "hearing voices in my head which tell me what to do" means that you're crazy, so people are unwilling to take a close look at where "their" thoughts are really coming from. Even people who aren't consciously aware of receiving messages from spirits nonetheless know that they experience hunches, inspirations, or dream messages that guide them in making decisions. Spirits are often the source of these communications.

Moreover, lots of people are possessed by spirits – both angelic and demonic ones, but in our society mostly the latter – whether they know it or not. Spirit possession is not a bad thing when the spirits involved are benevolent, like Jesus, Krishna, or Buddha.

This possession occurs when people invite a spirit to take possession of them. When Christians "make the decision for Jesus" or "invite Jesus to come live inside" them; or Buddhists "take refuge in the Buddha, Dharma, and Sangha"; they are inviting spirits to take possession of their souls. Possession by a good spirit fortifies people's faith and dedication to the spiritual path. It gives people backbone, something to rely upon in times of doubt.

However, these days demon possession is much more common than is possession by benevolent spirits. On a guess, the majority of people in our society are demon-possessed (certainly most of our leaders are; that's how they got to be our leaders). It's easiest to see that someone is demon-possessed when they get old, since by that time the demons have eaten up most of the people's souls and left uptight, angry or depressed, self-pitying, burned-out hulks in their stead. Life is a bitch, no question about it. However it tends to mellow out people who are not demon-possessed. Demon-possessed people, on the other hand, tend to get worse and worse the older they get.

People call demons in to possess them when they feel especially vulnerable and in need of drastic protection. For example, a baby may call in demons at birth to protect against abusive parents. Demons can be called in at any stage in life, usually unconsciously, to alleviate pain or sorrow by providing a protective shell of hardheartedness or self-pity. Luckily, it's not that hard to cast out demons. The hard part for demon-possessed people is wanting to cast them out in the first place.

When you channel spirits, you usually receive the information as thoughts or feelings. This is because thoughts and feelings are all you know; you don't know how to process information in any other fashion. However, that is not how the

What is Magic?

spirits themselves view this communication.[2] Moreover it is undoubtedly anthropomorphic to believe that spirits have sex (male or female) and personalities (jolly, somber, laid-back, strict, etc.). But that is how they appear to most people.

My own spirit guides are rather indulgent and soft, probably because I am indulgent and soft and get riled unless I am indulged and treated softly. On the other hand Mescalito, the spirit of the psychedelic peyote cactus, is cold, hard, and detached. I find him terrifying, in fact, although I still go to him on occasion. Mescalito doesn't indulge anybody.

In other words, spirits have different personalities, just as people do. They are not amorphous energies or something of the sort. Possibly it is a feature of human cognition that we apprehend spirits as having sex and personality, rather than that sex and personality are properties innate to the spirits themselves. This is similar to Carlos Castaneda's conundrum about psychic apprehension, what he termed *seeing*, being so visual, when it had nothing to do with vision whatsoever – whether his eyes were open or closed. But to him it seemed visual. His teacher don Juan's explanation of this was that humans come to magic as adults, with our perceptual biases already formed. Therefore when we learn a new form of cognition we tend to try to fit it into a familiar mold. Similarly, we tend to experience spirits' communications as thoughts or feelings, since these are our usual forms of communication. We relate to spirits' personalities because we are accustomed to relating to others through their personalities.

The easiest spirits to communicate with are your own spirit guides – what some people term "angels". More detailed information on what spirit guides are and how you can easily contact them is given in my book *Magical Living*. If you are serious about becoming a magician, then this is where you should start. The chief function of spirit guides is to act like cornermen in a boxing match: when you're completely exhausted and life has really knocked you for a loop, they're there to say: "You can do it! You're doing great! Just get back in there and go another round!"

How spirit guides teach depends on the person they are teaching. Sometimes they hand out information for free, particularly when they spot an opportunity that must be grasped at once. Because they see things with such clarity, guides can give detailed explanations of everything you might want to know about your life and relationships. Generally spirit guides are there to encourage you to figure things out and take responsibility for yourself. In my own case my guides use a lot of trickery, encouraging me to make an ass of myself, since this seems to be the only way I really learn anything.

Different spirits communicate in different ways. For example, my own spirit guides talk to me via automatic writing, in words in my head. It's just like having a conversation with another person, except that it's written rather than spoken. I can only hear my spirit guides talking to me when they're yelling at me for having screwed up somehow. My wife, who is much more psychic than I am, is able to hear them talking to her directly when she channels them. Another friend of mine, who is even more psychic than my wife, is able to hear them conversing amongst themselves.

I am a priest of the nine Mayan gods. When they have a message for me, they normally communicate with me in words in my mind, as my spirit guides do. However, when the message is for someone else – for me to give to another person, or for me about another person – then they usually show it to me indirectly, by means of omens. Omens are odd, unusual occurrences which have a symbolic meaning. My benefactress, the person who gave me the Mayan priesthood, has dreams in which the nine Mayan gods appear. She has told me that they appear to her as long-haired hippies. The only time one of the Mayan gods ever came to me in a dream he was wearing a three-piece suit.

However, Mescalito, the spirit of the peyote cactus, interacts with me on a much deeper level than my spirit guides or the Mayan gods do. I just know what Mescalito is communicating to me, even though there's nothing verbal about it. Somehow or other it comes from what I take to be a very, very deep level.

The one time the Virgin Mary appeared to me I only felt her presence. I didn't get a visual, nor did she speak. I had

What is Magic?

been looking for land to buy in a remote Mayan village, and as I walked around the village I was getting a lot of suspicion and bad vibes from the locals. My spirit guides suggested that I go to the marketplace and buy a candle, and light it in the village church before the image of the Virgin of Guadalupe. I was to ask her to make a place for myself amongst these people. When I did so I suddenly felt myself transported into the presence of a young woman – perhaps 20 years old at the most. This being was totally loving and compassionate, and she filled me with a sense of complete acceptance, nurturance, and joy. Ever since that day I've prayed to her every morning to help me open my heart (even though I'm nominally Jewish).

On various occasions religious statues in churches and temples have come to life momentarily before my eyes. Indeed, that is precisely what religious images are designed to do. If you are interested in communicating with spirits, praying to statues or images representative of the spirits of your religion can be a fruitful place to begin.

There are also nature spirits, such as mountain spirits, cave spirits, water spirits, tree spirits, and so forth. These spirits can be the most helpful of all to budding magicians. Where spirit guides guide, nature spirits can actually transform you. This is the crux of the spiritual path, the difference between momentary inspiration and real, permanent change. It has been said – for example by Buddhists and by Castaneda's teacher don Juan, that real transformation, true spiritual growth, is impossible without the help of a living, enlightened guru. This is true, but it's not true. Near-death experiences can do this for you in sudden fashion; and nature spirits can also do it for you in a slower, more relaxed manner. Nature spirits can actually get in there and work on you on your deepest, light fiber level, gently dissolving your lower self and liberating your true feelings.

Nature spirits, particularly cave and mountain spirits, often have powerful personalities. They should be approached with the greatest respect. Although every cave and mountain has a spirit, not all of these spirits are useful to humans. Sometimes such nature spirits are indifferent. At other times they are inimical to humans. For example, the San Pedro volcano on Guatemala's Lake Atitlan has happy, loving vibes. The town of San Pedro just beneath it is a light, happy place. But the next volcano over, Atitlan, is cold and hard and forbidding. The town of Santiago which lies beneath it is kind of an uptight place – famous for its black magicians and sorcery, and the scene of several massacres during and after the recent guerrilla war.

In order to make use of water spirits, it is first necessary to find them. This is not that hard to do. In an arid or semi-arid area, any water hole or spring will house a water spirit. Ponds, lakes, and oceans in their entirety can be considered to house one large spirit. Along rivers and streams you frequently find water spirits residing at spots where there are deep pools, waterfalls, rapids, or at bends in the river where there is a change in the vegetation or rock formations. Water spirits also reside at spots which are particularly lovely, different, attention-getting in some way or other; but basically you find them by feel – the physical appearance is just a clue or corroboration. Water spirits are used for washing off your self-importance: bad moods, self-pity, and negative vibes which other people lay on you.

Rock spirits are found in a similar way: by the feel of the way they look. The vortices around Sedona, AZ are a good example. Rock spirits can stabilize you and give you strength. This is good for athletes training for a contest or soldiers going to battle. Rock spirits also give fortitude – good for women who are weak in pregnancy. They also buttress your discipline, staying power, tenacity, and self-confidence. It's good to go to rock spirits when you need to be bolstered somehow; whereas water spirits are most useful when there's something you need to wash off.

You should feel an attraction to the place where a nature spirit resides. If you don't feel an attraction for the place, don't use it, no matter how extraordinary it may look. It's not that going to the wrong spirit will hurt you, although there are evil spirits out there. It's just that if you don't have an affinity with the spirit – feel a definite attraction or good feeling about the place – then it wouldn't be able to help you much. A doctor may be an excellent practitioner, but if he doesn't have

What is Magic?

an affinity with the patient then there's not much he can do for him. The same is true of spirits.

The physical appearance of the spot where a nature spirit abides is a useful check, but it shouldn't be allowed to be the only criteria. Just because a place looks gloomy or frightens you a little doesn't mean you shouldn't use it. Powerful spirits are always a bit frightening. They command respect, and will righteously punish disrespect. They can actually knock you around if you approach them in a casual or offhand way. A good friend of mine, a magician, was once climbing a spirit mountain with his baby daughter in his arms. Evidently the mountain spirit felt that his mood was disrespectful, since near the top there was a sudden clap of thunder out of a blue sky. My friend understood at once that he had blown it. He lost his footing and tumbled down. Since he was trying to protect the baby he couldn't protect himself, and he broke his collarbone in three places. Since then he hasn't been able to windsurf; and formerly he was the windsurfing champion of Central America. The point isn't that you must be in a dour, super-serious mood to visit power places and nature spirits. Rather, you must approach them with respect. That's all.

When you have found a likely nature spirit, i.e. when you feel that you're in the right place, approach the spirit by making an obeisance. Approach it as you would a wise old person whom you are asking to help you. You can take it a little present, such as flowers or some object meaningful to you. Try to feel the personality of that spirit, sense its energy. Is it an active, dominating male presence or a receptive, soothing female presence? Does it seem to be young and vigorous or old and placid? Some of the feeling is usually reflected in the physical appearance of the place. The spirit will tell you what to do there. Whatever it is that you feel you should do, go for it.

Pay close attention to all your thoughts and feelings when you are in the presence of a spirit. In the beginning it's difficult to tell which are your thoughts and feelings, and which are the spirit talking to you. After a bit of practice it's not hard to tell which is which. If you are in a relaxed, open state of mind in the presence of a nature spirit, then probably any thoughts or feelings you have are communications from the spirit. You would probably have regarded them as your own thoughts and feelings unless this fact were to be pointed out to you at the moment.

However, it doesn't really matter if you can consciously channel the spirit talking to you or not. This is actually a sidetrack, since the real healing work that nature spirits do has nothing to do with thoughts or feelings. They deal with you on a much deeper level than thoughts or feelings. So if you go to a nature spirit in good faith, with an open heart, the spirit's power will heal you with every visit.

Notes:

[1] For a different (and more detailed) view of what spirits are all about, see Allan Kardec's books (such as *The Spirits' Book*).

[2] Spirits see communication with humans (and humans' communication amongst themselves) as a mingling or bending of light fibers – an interaction within the aura, or shell of luminosity, which surrounds every being. In other words, spirits' cognition is very different from humans' normal, socially-conditioned mode of cognition. For example, spirits see time in terms of potentialities rather than concrete events.

III – Intent

The chief reliance that magicians use to further their intent and realize their desires is patience. Intent is a matter of waiting patiently for the *right* moment or *right* person to come along, instead of pushing to manipulate matters your own way, or grabbing the first thing that comes down the pike. The basic principle of magic can be summed up as: if you are antsy or smug, you are wrong, wrong, wrong – you are blowing your intent.

Intent is not a matter of running around like a chicken with its head cut off to make things happen. Nor is it just sitting back, hoping for the best, and letting things slide. Intent unfolds in the natural course of events. It's a matter of allowing things to develop naturally, and then acting decisively when the moment is right. Intent is a matter of knowing that you're in the hands of the Spirit – and that it is at your command.

Most of life consists of thought form blah-blah; but when magical events do happen, they happen very, very quickly. Everybody recognizes them in those split-second moments of truth (at least before they turn aside in fear and pretend that what just happened didn't happen). But average people are too focused on their importance agendas to be able to act on these impulses – to grab onto these light fibers (these gifts of energy from the cosmos). It requires being very light and nimble to be able to recognize these magical events when they occur (rather than pass mindlessly over them); and then to be able to grasp them in the now moment with no hesitation.

This is how the Jews returned to Palestine after two millennia of exile. They intended it, and intended it, and intended it patiently for two thousand years. Then, when the opportunity arose, they seized the moment and did everything possible through political and military channels – i.e. through normal means – to realize their intent. It isn't like Jehovah sent their messiah and miraculously split the sea for them to cross into the Promised Land. Not at all. Waiting on miracles is for losers.

This is also the way in which the Spirit does things. For example, when the Spirit decided that the time was right for life to appear on earth, it didn't up and create everything like pulling rabbits out of a hat. Rather the Spirit did it slowly, over zillions of years. The Spirit patiently prepared the earth and atmosphere and soup of chemicals until *ZAP!* – a lightning bolt smacked into the soup and *voila!* – there was a living cell. Then that cell began reproducing and eventually evolved into you and me (at least that's what the materialists say happened). The point is that even the Spirit can't command the universe by waving a wand and making things jump. The Spirit does things by intending them and then waiting patiently until a fortuitous juxtaposition of circumstances pops up. Then, and only then, does it act. This is precisely how you have to do things if you want to be a magician. You don't force things or bend them out of shape to get your own way. Rather, you intend your desire with all your heart, and then you wait patiently for the right moment to come along to further your intent. And then, and only then, do you pounce.

This is why spiritual change is so glacially slow. Here and there you reach a pinnacle of spiritual awareness, an epiphany, a breakthrough of realization and understanding. But then you always seem to drop back to the same old morass of your old, everyday self. Permanent spiritual growth *does* happen over time if you keep intending it, but it takes years and decades of pushing against the same unyielding wall – like isometric exercise – to see real results.

This is because spiritual growth *is* patience; you grow spiritually as you lose your sense of urgency and become willing to let things happen, rather than fluster around trying to make things happen. This is accomplished by exhaustion and burn-out rather than trying to run away from your karma somehow, as average people do. There's no other way (unless you have excellent karma to begin with – but then, look what happened to Jesus). But when transformation finally does happen, it happens very quickly; i.e., although importance is lost little-by-little over years and years, when it finally does run out, it runs out all at once. So if you feel you're not getting anywhere with your spiritual path; if you keep finding

What is Magic?

yourself back on square one; don't give up the faith. If you keep the faith long enough and patiently enough, finally you *will* fulfill your intent – your true purpose – the reason you were born.

This is how the ancient alchemists changed base metals into gold. They mixed their chemicals – the same chemicals – over and over and over, performing the exact same experiment thousands or tens of thousands of times, night after night, until finally it became gold. Of course in the process what they were doing was refining themselves. Refining the chemicals was symbolic of what was really going on inside them on an emotional and psychological level. So, too, is it with magicians. Being able to command the universe is symbolical of being able to command yourself. You create your own reality. You *are* your own reality. That is your base metal – the situation in which you find yourself right now. Intent means relaxing into your present circumstances, no matter how uncomfortable they may be, instead of cringing or clenching up against them and wishing they would go away. To command your circumstances you first have to be able to command yourself. This is the magician's creed.

It might be asked, what about all the people who seem to be able to get their way, to make their dreams come true, but who aren't particularly in command of themselves? What about all the nasties who get what they want? The answer is that some of these people are reaping good karma from past lives, and some of them are using black magic and the help of demons to get what they want. The latter is often the case when people rise from obscurity to great fame or worldly success, and then destroy themselves. However, being nasty is never the way to get what you want in your heart. You can't get love or peace that way, only sex, money, and applause. If sex, money, and applause are what you're after, then definitely black magic is better than white, and a lot less effort to boot. White magic requires not only patience, but wisdom. This wisdom means truly knowing your heart's desire – not what will bring you glory and make other people envy you. This is why most people can't get the so-called Law of Abundance to work – they don't know what they are really asking for. The essence of magic, at least white magic, isn't so much *getting* what you want but rather *knowing* what you want – in your heart of hearts, not your mind. It is what is in your heart of hearts – your intent – that creates your reality.

True intent cannot be developed by pursuing love or wealth or worldly success. True intent can only be developed when it is engaged in the service of an abstract purpose. The exact nature of that purpose doesn't really matter: to lose importance (what magicians do); to serve others selflessly (as Christians and Hindus do); or even to establish the free and unlimited coinage of silver at the ratio of sixteen to one. True intent must be developed for its own sake, as an end in itself, as art-for-art's-sake; without any personal expectations whatsoever driving it. True intent is developed by going the limit, by committing all your time, energy, and resources to something in which you have no personal stake at all (don't give a damn about the outcome).

Sometimes the coincidental nature of the outworkings of intent – such as fortuitous events, omens and portents – makes people believe that the Spirit has a personality, and especially that it cares about you personally. But omens don't originate in the Spirit (although Carlos Castaneda's teacher don Juan talks about them in that fashion); rather, they come from within the person experiencing them: they are part of that person's dream. Even though magicians sometimes refer to the Spirit's personality, such as that the Spirit sends omens, or that the Spirit is a trickster, in fact magicians know better. The Spirit is too vast to care, and you are too unimportant in the scheme of things to care about.

Conventional religions assign a personality to their God because most people are so embroiled in self-pity that they need a Great Pitying God to cry along with them. God is seen as some vast being who will intercede or intervene miraculously and save their butts so that they don't have to take responsibility for changing themselves. Society inculcates these sorts of belief systems into people to make them as dependent and acquiescent and fearful as possible.

The fact is that nothing in your life will change until you take upon yourself 100% of the responsibility for changing it.

What is Magic?

It's true that sometimes people pray to their God and get a miracle, but that is just a response to their own need to buck up their faith. They are the ones who brought that miracle about by their openness and willingness to rely on faith. God had nothing to do with it.

Intent operates slowly, in logical sequence. You pull yourself out of poverty by hard work. You find true love by becoming truly loving yourself. You heal yourself by understanding what lessons you are trying to learn from your illness and listening to what your body is telling you. In other words, whatever problems you have you solve through the application of patience. People who are desperately unhappy are actually in a much better position to utilize intent than are people who are merely unhappy: people who are merely unhappy are just seeking relief, whereas people who are desperately unhappy are seeking *change*.

There is a three-fold progression to intent: taking responsibility; confidence (faith); and success. Consider the intent of making money.

Taking responsibility means seeing clearly the mechanism involved: what you have to do to make money. This is simply a matter of dropping your self-pity, rolling up your sleeves, and getting to work, even if that means doing work that's 'beneath' you. Taking responsibility means doing whatever has to be done to address the realities of your situation; not necessarily what you would prefer doing. There's usually an important lesson to be learned here. What this entails is different in everyone's case, depending upon their individual situation.

Playing the lottery, however, is for losers. Anyone who's playing the lottery is buying into a loser's mindset. Money doesn't drop from heaven by magic. Rather, it comes to people who take responsibility. The way you drop your self-pity is by not wasting your intent buying lottery tickets, or watching television shows about the Lifestyles of the Rich and Famous, or reading the latest non-news about so-called celebrities, or fantasizing about wealth generally. All these sorts of activities feed self-pity. They are an actual drain on the energy needed to bring wealth.

Confidence, or faith, is also required. People who are lucky at attracting money know that the money will come. Even when they're broke or bankrupt, they know the money will come. It's a feeling in their bones. That confidence is what attracts money to them. In other words, it takes confidence to bring success: the much-vaunted Law of Abundance. Unfortunately, it takes success to bring confidence.[1]

Faith in magic doesn't spring from nothing. It isn't blind. Faith comes from seeing the techniques of magic actually work time and time again. When the principles involved are clearly understood and applied, the desired result is obtained. The problem is that in the beginning all you have to work with is blind faith since there aren't any results yet to base real faith on. Magicians get around this Catch-22 by using the technique of Creative Visualization. This technique is described in my books, and also in *Creative Visualization* by Shakti Gawain.[2]

Creative Visualization is a technique used to strengthen intent by hypnotizing yourself. C.V. is similar to daydreaming but has the opposite intent. Where daydreaming stokes self-pity, Creative Visualization strengthens intent. In normal daydreaming you are actually pushing away whatever object you are daydreaming about into a future which never comes. In Creative Visualization you are actively drawing the object of your visualization to yourself by imagining it physically happening in the now moment.

The difference between C.V. and normal daydreaming is that the former is a command of fulfillment and the latter is a command of lack. When you cling to someone or something – when you are needy – your actual intent is to drive them away. So many love songs contain the line, "I need you." But this is not love; this is lack. It is the same with fantasies, such as sex fantasies. These are commands of lack, not fulfillment. In Creative Visualization you imagine fulfillment right *now*.

The point is that true faith does not depend upon the realization of a particular expectation. Believing that your thought form images – your miraculous escape from your present circumstances into some ideal fantasy world – will

What is Magic?

come true, is not faith. It's fooling yourself. This is what most people spend their entire lives doing. Most people live for the daydream that someday the object of their fondest fantasies will drop into their laps from heaven with no effort on their part.

True faith, by contrast, is faith that everything is unfolding as it should; so be patient. True faith is the conviction that things will happen precisely as you, in your inmost heart, need for them to happen; so go with the flow. True faith is knowing that you can't control anything anyway, so you'd might as well quit worrying about it and just chill. Death will solve all your problems soon enough.

If you keep plugging away long enough in spite of setbacks, fears, and doubts, eventually success will come. The Dark Night of the Soul is part and parcel of success – you can't have one without the other. True faith holds fast, whereas phony faith evaporates and runs for safety or escape. True faith is forged in the fires of pain – burning off the dross. Of course, you can inherit wealth, for example, but that isn't success. Success – happiness – is something which you accomplish. It isn't something which you can inherit or which can be given to you.

Part of the mystery of intent is grace. If you reach out half way yourself, the Spirit will reach out for you the other half way and give you a lift. The Dark Night of the Soul is rarely as dark as your self-pity tries to make it. Or, as Otto von Bismarck put it: "Life is like being at the dentist's – you think that the worst is yet to come, but it's over already."

Although it is true that the Spirit is basically indifferent, it is nonetheless quite pliable. This is what is meant by "your intent becomes the Spirit's intent", to paraphrase Castaneda. In the monotheistic view God is outside of and above you, and dispenses or withholds goodies at His whim, or in response to your pressing or failing to press the correct lever, like Pavlov's dogs. In the pantheistic view you are the Spirit: your command becomes the Spirit's command. Therefore it is imperative to see clearly and precisely what it is that you are actually commanding.

For example, we all believe that we are pursuing happiness. This is a delusion. Happiness is a feeling you experience *now*. It is not something you can pursue. The pursuit of happiness is the pursuit of a mirage, like the mirage of water in a desert, which recedes as you seemingly get closer and closer to it. Happiness can only exist *now*. In order to be happy, then, you have to find things that will make you happy *now*, in the midst of your suffering. This is what the Birdman of Alcatraz did with his pet birds, and what Viktor Frankl did watching the sunset at Auschwitz.[3] You have to focus on those items of your everyday life which bring you happiness now, rather than focus on the things which bring you pain, or daydream about what you believe will alleviate your pain.

This is why it is an essential part of the practice of magic is to go out to nature, away from other people, every single day for at least half an hour. By choosing to focus your attention on that which brings you a sense of peace and plenitude, your sense of inner peace and plenitude enlarges. Eventually your intent moves the Spirit to change the outward circumstances of your life to reflect your new inner state of peace and plenitude. This is called grace.

The important point to remember is that you must do the inner work first. It's not like the outer circumstances of your life will change and then your suffering will be alleviated. Quite the contrary. This is why you find very few true magicians. Nobody wants to face this truth.

There are no shortcuts on the spiritual path. There is no lottery you can win, no dating service you can join, no instant cure for your chronic ailment, no spiritual master you can find who will wave a magic wand and suddenly make you happy. Consider the example of Carlos Castaneda. He was with an enlightened master for over a decade, yet when the master left Castaneda was about as screwed-up as when he began. Actually, it was only when don Juan left that Castaneda took the responsibility willy-nilly for putting together all he had learned and turned don Juan's teachings into a reality.

Commanding your intent, which starts from examining and then controlling your moment-to-moment thoughts, isn't something you do in one fell swoop. It happens little-by-little over years and decades of conscious effort. The only important thing is to intend it, to desire it with all your heart, and not stop intending it. This is the magic and mystery of intent. Even a weak intent, applied unremittingly over time, through thick and thin, acquires force. Turning the wheel of chance is a matter of unbending intent and infinite patience. That's all. With intent and patience eventually the wheel *will* turn.

Know in your heart that you always have a sword you can wield, and a solid rock you can stand on, to confront your destiny. That sword is intent and that rock is the now moment. It is the purpose of the practice of magic to hone the sword of intent to a keen edge.

Notes:

[1] When the solution to my life-long money problems finally did come, I saw it as "I received a bunch of money, and as a result I am now happy." That's how it seemed to me at the time. But my guides have told that I'm wrong, that it's a common mistake to make, but actually it was my own loss of money importance (obsessive concern over money) which brought about the "outside" event which gave me that wonderful feeling of relief from poverty after many, many years of financial limitation. That by just shrugging my shoulders in acceptance of my money problems, by stopping pitying myself for my money problems, I had given myself permission to move past them.

[2] Gawain, Shakti, *Creative Visualization*, Bantam NYC 1982

[3] Frankl, Viktor, *Man's Search for Meaning*, Beacon Press, Boston 1992.

IV – The Nature of Reality

It's difficult to understand what magic is without understanding the nature of the self and reality. This is not an irrelevant question which is best relegated to Philosophy 101 – meaningless, empty talk which philosophers debate about endlessly to no purpose. Rather, understanding what the self and reality really are cuts to the very heart of magic. It's a question of everyday life, of where you focus your moment-to-moment attention. It is by scrutinizing this question and not allowing themselves to be fooled by superficial appearances that magicians obtain whatever advantage they have over most people (not by supernormal powers). It's a sad commentary on the state of our society that the antics of so-called celebrities, and the latest fashions, buzz-words, and gadgets, are much more important to most people than the questions, "Who am I?", "What am I?", and "What the hell is going on here?"

A fundamental principle of magic is that reality – what you experience when you are awake – is but a specialized form of dreaming. Dreaming came first evolutionarily, and being awake is a later adaptation, rather than vice versa. You believe that what you experience when you are awake is real. However, it is also true that you believe that what you experience when you are asleep is real – at least while you are still dreaming. It is merely the belief that what you are experiencing is real that makes it real. This seems to be a very difficult point for people to understand. You indeed create your own reality. There is no outside reality impinging upon you, in spite of superficial appearances to the contrary. What you experience as the outside world, or reality, is no more real than the dreams you had last night.

Why then does the world that you experience while you are awake seem so real? This is due to your constant thinking, your constant inner dialogue, which holds your waking reality together for you. If your self-referent thinking should ever stop, so too would your reality

What is Magic?

If you objectively examine the contents of your inventory of habitual thoughts you will discover that most of them consist of thoughts of glory – receiving approval and approbation from other people; and shame – hatred of your looks, your actions, and your feelings. Glory and shame are two sides of the same coin: the me-me-me coin. If you stop thinking these thoughts, then the "me" – the sense of a separated, continuing self who is alternately exalted and debased – ceases as well. When this lower self collapses, so too does the so-called real world.

There are other societies, magical societies, in which people don't think as much as we do. The reality the members of these societies experience in their daily lives is more magical than ours is. The world of the Mayan Indians of Guatemala is a good example. Freidel-Schele-Parker, in their book *Maya Cosmos*,[1] contrast the Spanish and Mayan worldviews through their respective descriptions of the decisive battle in which Pedro Alvarado defeated Tecun Uman, the leader of the Kiche Maya, on February 22, 1524:

"According to Alvarado, this was just another battle among many. In a letter to Cortez, he said that several thousand Kiche warriors approached his troops while they were taking a break for food and water. They let the Indians close the distance. Then they attacked and routed the Indian army, pursuing them until they were trapped against a mountain. ... He mentioned that one of the Kiche chiefs was killed, but he did not even record his name. The Kiche account is told as if a totally different series of events had unfolded."

In the Kiche Mayan version, the battle was between the magic and gods of the Mayan Indians and the magic and gods of the Spanish: the Virgin Mary and her attendant angels. In the Kiche version, Tecun Uman assembled an army of 8000 warriors to oppose the 700-man Spanish army, then he used magic to transform himself into an eagle and flew against Alvarado, but "he could not kill him because a very fair maiden defended him; they were anxious to enter, but as soon as they saw this maiden they fell to the earth and they could not get up from the ground, and then came many footless birds, and those birds had surrounded the maiden, and the

Indians wanted to kill the maiden and those footless birds defended her and blinded them."

Whose version of the battle is correct? The Spanish themselves credited their God and the protection of the Virgin Mary with their stunning victories against overwhelming odds, even if they weren't able to get the same visual take on the thing that the Maya got. Modern historians, whose worldview is even less magical than the sixteenth century Spanish view, try to explain the outcome in purely materialistic terms. From the magicians' point of view, none of these views are correct; or rather, they all are, because people create their own realities based on what their social training and personal experience of the world have led them to expect. The reason why most modern people experience so little magic in their lives is because they've trained themselves to be closed-up and insensitive, and to expect life to be routine and dull.

Our constant thinking, and the customary moods and concerns which this thinking conjures up, is a screen which keeps our intuitive perception of the world under wraps. Without this screen the world becomes vivid and magical, teeming with life and meaning. My book *Magical Living* describes a simple technique for following feelings and for opening yourself to the magic of the world. When following feelings you shift from the closed-up mindset of thinking (conceptual) awareness into a state of enhanced (sensory) awareness in which you can feel what plants are feeling, sense emanations of power from the earth, interact with spirits, and so on. The world of enhanced awareness is a world of constant surprises and delight. However you couldn't balance a checkbook or interview effectively for a job in this state. The point is that what blocks your magical perception of the world is your fear; and your anger; and your fear of your anger; and your anger at your fearfulness; etc. etc. That is your constant inner dialogue. That is the reality which you have created for yourself.

In actual fact, there is *nothing* out there whatsoever. Zilch. Reality actually consists of nothingness. Any reality which you perceive is your own invention: a gloss over the basic stuff of the universe, which is void. The Buddhists call

What is Magic?

this *Shunyata*, or emptiness. It's sort of like the fact that a movie is actually colored celluloid with light passing through it. Now if you can go one step further and imagine that even the colored celluloid and light don't exist either, then you've got a picture of what's really going on. God doesn't exist; the universe doesn't exist; existence doesn't exist. This happens to be the truth; but since truth doesn't exist either, we may as well just let the subject lay.

Magic, in fact, is the only logical, reasonable, rational worldview since it is completely illogical, unreasonable, and irrational. An important principle of magic is that magic is a false view of reality, since reality can't be viewed. It cannot be comprehended with the mind, by thinking. It can, however, be glimpsed with the feelings, by direct knowing. It can be apprehended with intuition and acted upon with intent.

It is important to understand what the self really is if you expect to understand what reality is. The myth of a separated lower self – a body; and the myth of an external reality impacting upon that body; arise together. These are two ways of looking at the same basic falsehood. In actual fact you are not separated from the world, and the world is not outside of you.

What fools you is your linear view of time. You mistakenly believe that things happen to you, and then you react to them (as I did when a fortuitous injection of cash solved my longstanding money problems). For example, first you get laid off from your job, and then you feel depressed and helpless. However from the magical point of view, the decision to feel depressed and helpless is primary – is made "first". The getting laid off is conjured up "later" to justify your feelings of self-pity. Face it: there are lots of options – feelings you could conceivably feel in any given situation. For example, if you get laid off you could just as easily feel relieved, glad that one's over, hopefully looking forward to a new career. The choice to feel self-pity about what happens to you is always a free choice. The choice to feel self-pity at the things which happen to you – as if you didn't bring them to you in the first place – is what creates the illusion of a separated self at odds with an outside reality. What you consider your self is just your self-pity. Since this point is the entire basis of magical training, it bears repeating: the lower self is nothing more than self-pity, and when self-pity is eradicated the lower self dissolves also.

If you're going to understand and act on this point of view, you have to get over your prejudice, which is all it is, about time being linear. The fact is that time is not linear. Survivors of near-death experiences often report having seen every single event that ever happened to them during their lives flash by them in no time at all. Sometimes they report seeing everything that ever happened to them zip by, but still being able to see each scene discretely, in a few seconds' time. Others report seeing each individual event of their entire lives in one, complete take. In any case, it would seem that you experience the thought forms of your life twice: once in linear fashion over a lifetime, and then in a non-linear fashion at the moment of your death.

This idea that time can be non-linear is easiest to see in dreams. Dream time is sequential, but not linear in the same sense in which waking time is linear. Dream time doesn't have the same cause-and-effect inexorability that waking time has. This is because there is less importance (self-pity) present in dreaming, so everything is more here-and-now. You don't feel moods and concerns as acutely in dream time as you do when you're awake because you don't think so much. Things happen too fast and too intensely in dreams to dwell upon. Everything is just too vivid and too now.

Infants and young children are basically doing what we adults would consider dreaming even while awake. Being awake – and the sense of linear time – are something you learn as you grow up. That's why it seems to you that childhood lasted forever (while you were still a child): because your sense of the linear passage of time wasn't yet fully formed. Linear time is a byproduct of your ability to think; and if you can't think (or don't think) then time becomes eternity.[2]

In life-threatening situations, such as while you are having an automobile accident, or during a big earthquake, time slows way down. You can see everything that is happening with great clarity, in great detail, as if it were

What is Magic?

unfolding in slow motion. This slow motion perception of time is closer to the truth. It is more like dream time perception and less like normal, everyday, gloss-over-things-quickly-and-superficially perception of time. However, most people are incapable of acting in the normal way in this slow motion perception of time because they can't think. If you are going to act or react in this frame of mind, you can only do so on intent, on gut-level instinct, not on thought. Therefore the slow motion perception is not as useful in performing all the humdrum tasks of everyday life as is normal time perception; but it is the more useful form of perception in the practice of magic, where decisions have to be made faster than normal thinking allows.

When time slows down enough you lose your sense of separated selfhood and move into altered states of consciousness. Indeed, "timelessness" is how people usually describe such states. Altered states can occur due to shock, psychedelic drugs, or even spirits. Some spirits have the power to temporarily erase your self-pity so that you experience a state of selfless grace. Enlightenment is such a state – people who are enlightened can move into and out of timelessness and selflessness at will, by focusing their attention one way or the other.[3] But even enlightened people don't exist in a state of nirvana all day long. They have normal lives to lead too, and altered states are not particularly functional in everyday society.

Normal, everyday life is the battleground, the place where the real work has to be done, the place where it all begins and ends. Altered states can be inspiring, can give you a glimpse of the goal you are shooting for, but they are always temporary. The goal is to bring an awareness of timelessness and selflessness into the routines of your everyday life. You do this by detaching from your self-important, self-pitying me-me-me with its endless fluster of moods and concerns.

The essential tenet of magic is that you create your own reality. This means that the things which happen to you are attracted by your moods and concerns. It's only by controlling your moods and concerns, your thinking, that you can control your reality. Of course, this is a lot easier said than done.

Your moods and concerns have a tremendous momentum of their own. To turn back that tide means to literally rewrite your personal history and to let go of the past, and to release your expectations and let go of the future.

There are ways of doing this. Life kicking the crap out of you until you're totally burned out is the easiest way, if you consciously use it to lose self-pity rather than stoke self-pity (as average people do). Of formal magical techniques one of the most powerful and effective is recapitulation (explained in my book *The Great Wheel*), which involves reliving your memories to discharge the energy pent up in them. There are also many other techniques for self-transformation. These usually take years and years of dedicated practice before you start seeing concrete results: controlling your reality by controlling your moods and concerns and your moment-to-moment thinking.

The purpose of Creative Visualization is to take a short-cut to creating your own reality, without all the years of work. We'll describe this technique in future chapters, particularly the chapters on *Spells, Charms and Rituals* and *Bewitching*. The point is that the difference between the magician's reality and average people's reality is that the magician makes a thoughtful, informed choice of what his or her reality will be. Most people, on the other hand, accept their lives at face value and question nothing that they were taught. Neither is right or wrong, it's all *Shunyata*, emptiness; but one choice leads to freedom, and the other leads to slavery.

Notes:

[1] Freidel, David; Schele, Linda; Parker, Joy; *Maya Cosmos*, William Morrow NYC 1993 page 328.

[2] *"Eternity is not a long time but a short time. ... Eternity is in the glitter on the beetle's wing."* – William Butler Yeats

[3] Buddhists aver that experienced meditators can slow time down enough so as to be able to discern individual

thought forms (*sankhara*), moods (*sanna*), and desires (*vedana*), at the instant they arise.

V – Spells, Charms, and Rituals

Spells are the same thing as prayers, but not necessarily directed towards a deity (although they can be). The reason why a magician's spells are usually more efficacious than most people's prayers is not because magicians have any special innate powers. Rather, it's because their intent is more realistic. Most people pray for their desires to come true; whereas magicians pray to be shown how to make their desires come true.

Another reason why most people's spells don't work is because they haven't developed the sensitivity to understand that the little coincidence; or offhand remark someone made; or person they happened to bump into; or other little "cubic centimeter of chance" which popped up in the hours or days after casting their spell; was in fact their spell coming true. Very rarely does the Spirit announce its gifts with trumpets blaring. What usually happens is that people cast their spells or make their prayers and the Spirit brings them an opportunity; but the people are too blinded by their preconceived images, or are in too much of a hurry, to see that their spell did in fact come true (brought them exactly what they were asking for); but they ignored or rejected it.

Most people believe that things just happen; or that an omnipotent God could make things happen if you could somehow fake God out. Magicians believe that they must take full responsibility for making their desires come true. That's what intent is – taking full responsibility, leaving nothing whatsoever to chance. That's why magicians are never disappointed when their desires don't come true, because they did their best, and that's all they can do. It's like the Native Americans who fought against the encroaching whites, or the Jews in the Warsaw ghetto who fought the Germans, knowing all along they had no chance to win. It wasn't the winning that ultimately mattered – and it's not the winning that ultimately matters to a magician, but rather doing your best (although there are probable realities in which the Native Americans and Jews in Warsaw did win out in the end).

What is Magic?

Most people are addicted to some fantasy like winning the lottery, or marrying Mr. or Ms. Right, or meeting a true guru, and then all their problems will be over. These kinds of fantasies are useful in that they can provide a feeling of hope, false though it may be, to help get through the really hard times. However, addiction to such fantasies tends towards irresponsibility. It dissipates the very intent needed to find true happiness in life. Permanent change requires hard work and infinite patience. The final stroke of success may occur suddenly and even unexpectedly, but the preparation and toil take years and years. That's the difference between the magicians' way and average people's way. Average people are looking for a quick fix and a free ride, whereas magicians know there ain't no such thing.

In the popular American television program *Charmed*, the witches have a book of shadows which conveniently contains specific spells for every single situation, no matter how outlandish, that they encounter. However, while spells do exist and do work, it's not quite as simple as it appears in *Charmed*.

To make spells work it is necessary to understand what expectation is, and its relation to intent. That is to say, how you make things happen or not happen, the mechanism by which you create your own reality.

People trying to understand the spiritual path sometimes wonder that, if you lose your desires as many spiritual paths seem to advocate, what spice or zest does life have left? In fact, it's not desire per se that spiritual seekers try to eradicate, but rather expectation. Expectation means taking things personally, caring about what happens. It isn't so much spice and zest that are lost as urgency and grasping. The things that average people care about do indeed lose their zest and spice; but in return things like the sound of the wind whispering in the trees and the feel of its caress on your skin become exquisitely piquant, sensual, and exciting.

When most people lose their expectations, which usually occurs because something they had a lot of stake in crashes, they experience this as depression. To depressed people life is indeed an empty, meaningless wasteland with no purpose or reward. Having lost the expectations which underpin their sense of self-worth and self-esteem, they feel they have also lost all sense of purpose, or intent. Actually, depressed people are very, very close to enlightenment if they only knew it. Their problem is that usually they are demon-possessed, and their demons are blocking their vision with self-pity.

Magicians, on the other hand, deliberately seek to crash their expectations, since they know that this is the path to freedom. Losing your expectations is the only way to center yourself in the now moment instead of being trapped by the yearning for a future which never comes. True self-esteem is a matter of permitting yourself to be happy *now*, of being able to truthfully say to yourself: "What's happening right this minute is okay by me. I don't need to have this, that, or the other in order to be happy; and I don't need to prove this, that, or the other in order to be a worthwhile person." It's a matter of getting off your own case and other people's cases; and off God's case.

The way expectations are normally lost is by having them crash, and crash, and crash. There's really no short-cut, no other way (a near-death experience can do the job quickly, but that's not everyone's karma). If you bang your head futilely against the same wall over and over again, you finally arrive at a point of exhaustion, and you collapse on the ground in despair. At that point, the moment of finally giving up your own will, you look around and usually you can see a clear path in another direction that is open and free of obstructions. The point is that the feeling of being blocked, or trapped on the same treadmill of frustration, is a message that – for whatever reasons – you are going about things incorrectly. When you give up your self-will you usually are able to understand what that message is, to see quite clearly why you had been blocked previously.

It is necessary to lose all expectation before you can find true happiness. For example, most single people think that what they want is a relationship, but this is misguided. "A relationship" – in the abstract – is an expectation. It's not a relationship with a real, live person. Is a relationship with the wrong person what you want? Where you have to try to force them to fit an image you have which is not who they really are? Wouldn't you rather be alone than in a relationship in which there is bickering and lying and betrayal happening? Surely it is better to wait until the right person comes along than to try to grab candidates off the street and bribe or coerce them into a relationship. And if the right person never comes along, so be it. Since you create your own reality, there must be some lesson or reason for your solitude. The point is to just try to be happy now, alone, instead of expecting some stranger to come along and make you happy. Unless you're happy now, who would want to hook up with such a sourpuss? So the best way to attract a relationship is to work on your own happiness. This doesn't mean you have to stop wanting a relationship in order to make one happen – just stop obsessing over it. Do you remember things that you desperately wanted when you were a child that you don't give a hoot about anymore? It's like that. By not caring so much whether you're in a relationship or not, by not making your happiness depend on it, is how to make a relationship happen. Going to the trees and nature spirits every day is the actual technique used to accomplish this feat.

The way to achieve your desires is to release the pressure of expectation by lightening up. This is why dilettante magicians can't get their spells to work properly, and also why most people's prayers don't work. They can't just send a powerful intent out there and then drop it. They worry and fret and examine whether this is happening or that is happening. They don't hold it all inside. What they're doing instead is frittering their intent away in self-pity. It's when you stop caring so much one way or the other, allowing events to unfold naturally and letting other people make the moves rather than acting on your own accord, that things start coming through for you (en passant: this is pretty much impossible to do as an act of will unless you are enlightened already. This is why you need an outside agent such as a truly enlightened guru, or nature spirits, to transform you).

It's difficult to describe the difference between eager expectation, which is akin to naïve fantasy, and eager anticipation, which leads to your desires being realized, since they both feel rather alike. But with eager anticipation every little thing that happens – except, of course, out-and-out bad stuff – every gust of wind, the sound of leaves rustling, the sight of a pretty color, makes you happy and gives you a little rush of joy. Conversely, with eager expectation, only the things which seem to advance the fulfillment of your specific expectations bring you joy.

Happiness can not, should not, does not depend on the fulfillment of an expectation. Expectation pushes happiness away indefinitely. Happiness is something you feel, or don't feel, as the case may be, right now. This means finding something that's going on this very minute which is joyous and fulfilling. Stop reading a minute and take a deep breath. Go look out the window. If all you see is bricks, look up at the clouds. The only way you are ever going to be happy is to find something that is going on right this minute which gives you a little lift. Even a teensy lift in the midst of horrendous suffering is a good beginning. Then you have to work at expanding that feeling. There's no other way, no shortcut to happiness. This is what magicians mean by taking responsibility for making your own happiness. Rolling up your sleeves and getting down to work is what entices the Spirit to reach out to you and give you a hand. This is how to make your spells work: by controlling your attitude. There's no way to fake this. It's accomplished by painstaking inner work and daily visits to nature spirits over many years of time.

The difference between rituals and spells is that rituals are to invoke spirits, whereas spells are to accomplish something specific. Spells are for us, to accomplish our own ends. Rituals are for the spirits, to provide an opening or channel into this world through which spirits can realize their own intent. When you perform a ritual to invoke spirits in good faith, rest assured that they come. They may not come with bells and whistles, but they come, whether you are consciously aware of their presence or not. Therefore rituals and invocations shouldn't be done frivolously.

Once I was leading a Jewish passover seder. Like most traditional church rituals, such as the Roman Catholic mass, the seder is an invocation of spirits. I had neglected to leave

What is Magic?

the customary place at the table for Elijah. When we arrived at that part of the seder service where the door is opened for Elijah to come in, I felt a definite presence enter the room, and that presence was quite ticked off at having been called without having been served at the table. The moral is, if you're going to invoke spirits, be respectful and aware of what you're about.

Some kids under the influence of satanic rock music who invoke demons "just for fun" are in for a big surprise later in life, when the demons exact payment. These people may never be consciously aware of the fact that their fooling around with demons as kids is what brought them the ill-health and ill-luck they face as adults. In other words, there's no such thing as fooling around with the invocation of spirits, whether beneficent or maleficent. Beneficent spirits don't like being treated disrespectfully, and invoking them frivolously tends to make them angry. Any invocation of a spirit is the real thing and has consequences.

Sometimes people who have old books on spirit invocation ask me to invoke the spirits for them. My reply is that people should invoke spirits themselves. There's nothing I can do that people can't do for themselves. Usually these sorts of books give complete instructions on how the spirits should be invoked: propitious days, times, what seal should be drawn in the magic circle and in what colors, what words should be spoken, and so forth. This is all the information anyone needs to invoke particular spirits for particular purposes.

However I am reluctant to invoke unknown spirits, unless directed to by my own spirit guides. While there are indeed spirits who can bring you financial help, romance, take vengeance on your enemies, and so forth, these sorts of spirits – albeit not demons per se – often exact considerable payment in return for their favors. There aren't any freebies out there in the universe. So be careful what you get involved with. Definitely consult your own spirit guides before invoking outside spirits.

The story on spells and charms is this: store-bought amulets and books of spells are pretty much worthless. It isn't the trinkets or the words that matter, but rather the intent behind them. It's better that you write your own Creative Visualizations rather than borrow someone else's. Similarly robes, magical tools, incense, and similar trappings don't matter in the least. If you like such things, however, feel free to use them. These objects can be useful in imbuing the moment you cast a spell or ritually invoke a spirit with a sense of importance, and help to put you in the right mood. Just remember that the magical clothes, tools, and chants are irrelevant. The only thing that matters is intent.

I purchase my charms in a local Mayan Indian market. They're nothing special by themselves – sort of like what you would find for sale in an occult shop. What makes them special is that I place them on the altar when I do rituals to invoke my patron spirits, and then these spirits bless the charms. You can also take your charms to any local nature spirit or power place to be blessed. I regard blessing a charm as similar to formatting a diskette. The charm is now ready for use, but still has to be written to, or charged with the particular intent or use to which it will be put. A charm or amulet is a physical representation of a spell. Charms can be worn around the neck or on a bracelet, or carried in a pocket or purse. They act as a reminder or protection, depending upon the purpose with which they were charged. Charging charms and amulets is best done during a relevant planetary hour.

Curses are the same thing as prayers, but with a negative intent. Because curses are the product of our fellow humans, they are much more difficult to cast off than are demons. Humans are far more ornery and vexatious than are demons, who are relatively straightforward and aboveboard by comparison.

One of the more interesting (and quite common) curse-related phenomena which I've seen is the way in which black magicians can place curses on person A to take to person B, so that A and B start fighting amongst themselves. I did something similar once when I was bewitching a woman for love – putting light fibers of desire on the woman's roommate to take to her. At the time I was vaguely aware that I was doing this, but I can't explain how I did it; nor could I repeat it

What is Magic?

at will (I only did it that one time). I don't think I was doing this on my own hook, but rather was being cued by the spirits I was working with (just as black magicians are cued by the demons who possess them). A lot of magic is done by spirit helpers – not by the magicians themselves (who basically just follow their spirits' cues).

The point is that often the black magic of people putting curses on one another is done unconsciously. Since in our society people are taught to disbelieve in magic, the result is that all that magic is still happening, but the people stupidly refuse to acknowledge and take responsibility for what is going on right in front of their eyes. By contrast in magical societies such as Guatemala, if someone suffers a run of coincidental "bad luck", they immediately start considering who might be responsible for same (who wishes them ill).

My benefactress, who is a priestess of the nine Mayan gods, has told me that curses should be removed by a professional, and not attempted alone if you don't know what you're doing. She removes curses as follows:

You can't do it without prayer. Say whatever prayer is appropriate to your faith – e.g. you could use the Our Father – into each radial pulse three times while burning copal (or any acrid incense, such as patchouli) around the person. Then say it three times over the forehead. You may have to repeat these nine prayers a few times until you feel the pulse calm down. You also need a spiritual bath with various herbs. We use nine for this: pipers, marigold, rue, life everlasting, all collected with prayers of thanksgiving and faith. Mash all the leaves in a bucket of water and set it in sun for a few hours. When the person comes, say the prayers, burn the copal and bathe their aura and physical body with the bath water.

My teacher don Abel Yat (a Mayan daycounter) removed curses by having the subject take special baths for thirteen days. The person must abstain from sex during this period, and each evening take a normal shower. After the shower, the person pours a pot of tea made from special plants boiled together and cooled down over him or herself (the plants are wild marigold, rue, and *chilka* – a local plant thought to bring luck; with three shredded cigars and an eighth of *aguardiente* liquor mixed in). After the ceremonial bath two candles are lit and the subject prays for forgiveness and liberation from the curse.

I've had curses put on me, more than once in fact, in the course of some unfortunate run-ins with a black witch. After smoking cigarettes for many years I eventually developed a constant emphysematous cough which no doctor I went to could help me with. Finally I went to a Huichol shaman in Mexico who asked me to give him a candle to burn at night, to see if he could find the answer to my problem in a dream. The next morning he told me that he had seen that someone – he didn't know who, but I did – had put a curse on me. The curse had resided in my weakest place, my lungs. The shaman had me return to him several times, each time making passes over my body with feathers. He prayed and sucked something out of the top of my head and spit it into his fireplace. He gave me a decoction of herbs and peyote to drink, and prescribed a special cleansing diet for a week. On my last visit he had me open my right palm and placed a cross in it, and then had me clasp my left hand over it. At that instant a glass with a candle burning in it on the altar behind us shattered with a loud "CRACK!" and I knew at that moment that the curse had left me.

It is often said that Creative Visualization and prayer should be done with the certain conviction that your desire is already realized: that what you're visualizing or praying for is already true. The question arises, how can you fervently believe that your desire is true when the overwhelming physical evidence is to the contrary? For example, how can you convince yourself that you are in radiant good health when all the logical signs point to your dying of cancer?

In casting spells, or making prayers or doing Creative Visualizations, which are all basically the same thing, what you are trying to do is to coax a sense of abundance from within yourself. You look out at the exact same landscape that you are seeing now – of being impoverished, or lonely, or sick – and yet you try to find meaning, worth, and purpose in it. Trying to conjure up a sense of fulfillment and self-worth in

What is Magic?

the midst of misery is a trick of magic. It isn't easy, but it can be done. Is this lying to yourself? No more so than believing that God is going to wave His magic wand and take away all your troubles.

The way that you build faith that your desire will indeed come true is by seeing it unfold in omens and portents. These are dress rehearsals of your desire being realized; or at least signs that the impersonal forces of the universe are listening. This is the difference between knowing with certainty that your desire will come true, as opposed to vaguely hoping that someday it will drop down from heaven by magic. When you have true faith you can see it all coming together in omens and portents, and can guide it along. You can see what you have to do now to get from here to there, instead of running around half-cocked frantically trying this and that to make your desires come true. For example, magicians don't choose their own partners or teachers (much less scour around looking for them). Magicians wait for the Spirit to bring them a partner or teacher when the time is right; and they recognize who and when by the omens. Omens only "speak" when expectation – phony faith – is erased. With true faith it's a matter of increasing joy and confidence as you go along, instead of riding a constant roller coaster of inflated hopes and crushing disappointments, and repeating the same stupid mistakes over and over. True faith is never blind. It's based on having seen positive results in the past.

It is best to cast a spell or perform a ritual during a planetary hour propitious for the purpose of that spell or ritual.[1] However planetary hours are merely a help, not a necessity. Once you have found a propitious time to cast your spell, you must consider the form that it will take. Write down ahead of time exactly what you want, so that you don't forget anything when the time comes. However, it's best not to be too specific in what you're asking for, such as to win the lottery, or to have such-and-such a person fall in love with you. It's best just to ask for wealth, or love from some unnamed person. Let the Spirit handle the details – it knows what it's doing.

When casting a spell it is important to address the real issue, rather than the presenting problem. For example, recently I was casting a spell to bring money (during a Jupiter planetary hour the day before a sun – Jupiter conjunction). As I was lighting the candle I realized that it wasn't money qua money that I wanted, but rather the free time to write what I want to write, instead of having to spend most of my time doing menial work, which I have to do to get by economically. So, on the spot I changed my prepared spiel to a visualization of living in a remote place in nature where I have the freedom to write – write – write to my heart's content without interruption.

I usually cast spells at power places or power trees, but you can make an altar in a corner of a room. Prepare your altar with something that symbolizes the Spirit above it. This can be a picture of Jesus if you're a Christian, or just a cut-out picture of an eye, or whatever symbolizes the Spirit for you. Put a stick of sweet-smelling incense on the altar, and a candle whose color symbolizes what you're asking for: green for money, pink for love, white for health or spiritual illumination, and so forth. Also put on the altar objects which symbolize what you want: money if you want money; cut-out pictures of lovers in love if you want love; pictures of healthy, active people if you want health; a photo of yourself from a time in your life when you were happy if you want happiness; and so forth.

Just prior to the chosen time light the incense. Then, at the precise moment chosen for the spell, light the candle. Then call upon the Spirit to grant your wish. It's okay to read it, but you should do this with feeling – true longing for whatever it is that you want. Picture in your mind's eye your desire coming true as you call for it; imagine the scene is unfolding all around you this minute; and let yourself feel all the joy you would feel if this were really happening. Lose yourself in joy. Don't worry about whether you are doing it right: if you're doing it in good faith with true longing, then you're doing it right. You get better at making it vivid with a little practice.

What is Magic?

If you have difficulty visualizing the object of your desire coming true right now, then something is blocking the prayer or spell. If you are casting a spell for money, for example, imagine how much you actually *need* (not necessarily how much you *want*) in terms of hundreds, thousands, 10,000's, or whatever. Then make grabbing gestures towards the candle flame, first with one hand and then with the other, in alteration. With each grab imagine taking a handful of one hundred, one thousand, or whatever, dollars; and then stuff it into your pocket. Continue this grabbing and stuffing, counting as you go. When you feel a resistance – a block – at that number of hundreds or thousands or whatever you have counted to, you will receive that much money, and no more. Note that in casting spells to bring money, it is more efficacious to ask for a specific amount of money to accomplish a specific purpose, rather than to imagine yourself surrounded by luxury and indolent pleasures of the flesh. That is *daydreaming*, not *visualization* – thinking, not feeling. Daydreaming is what losers do – they idly fantasize undeserved glory. Visualization is what winners do – they see an actual future out there, and they dynamically draw that probable reality to themselves by opening that door (giving themselves that permission).

If you are casting a spell to remove disease from your body, then pass each of your hands over the flame alternately, and imagine pulling vitality from the flame into your hands. Then pass your charged hands gently over the part of your body which needs healing and discharge the flame's healing energy into it. Then, with a determined grasping gesture, grab the illness from that part of your body and cast it out decisively with a sharp snap of the wrist. This is how you can make a spell to heal yourself – or to bring a healer who can help you.

Watch the candle closely for an omen of how your wish will go. If it is difficult to light the candle, then it will be difficult to make your wish come true. If the flame wavers, is feeble, or dies, then the wish probably won't materialize. If the flame burns tall and brightly, then the wish will come true; and the bigger and brighter the flame, the more assured and wonderful the outcome. However if the candle should fall over, forget it (this usually means that you're screwing up somehow; or there's pretty heavy karma in the way that you aren't taking into account). Also watch for unusual occurrences while you are casting your spell: for example, the sudden appearance of singing birds (if you are outside) or shafts of sunlight suddenly appearing through the clouds. These sorts of things are good omens for your wish coming true.

When performing a Scat ritual to get rid of some unwanted person from your life or to cast out demons, if you are e.g. attacked by a horde of insects, or stumble and fall and hurt yourself, shortly after casting your spell, then this is a good omen (the meaning is that the person's demons are striking back at you; therefore your spell worked). Note that this is true only of Scat-type rituals; in most other circumstances such happenings are decidedly evil portents.

In general, the ideal flame is bright throughout. If there are dark spots, this can indicate hidden problems such as illness (if the candle represents a person, then dark spots indicate illnesses or emotional problems), treachery, or other underlying difficulties. Two dark spots show two problems, or two problematical persons, blocking the desire. A bright, strong flame with large dark spot inside means that the question or desire will have a favorable outcome, but there is something else going on which will undermine it.

If you are able to see auras (it is much easier to see candle auras than human auras), then observe the color of the aura surrounding the flame as well as the behavior of that flame in interpreting the omen. The color will indicate something about the person (if the candle represents someone) or the question (if the candle represents a desire or prayer) which is going on in the background. The colors have the usual meanings: pink shows affection, red shows lust / anger, yellow shows intellect, white shows spirituality, black shows blockages, etc. You read the flame and aura according to what the candle is for, e.g. in a health matter, the flame represents the body (and any dark spots in it show roughly what part of the body is affected), and the auric color shows the

What is Magic? 63

background cause of the illness, or the eventual outcome. The flame gives the answer and indicates people or events involved; the aura shows the karmic conditions.

Remember that the thing has to be done by *feeling*, not thinking: it's not the behavior of the flame that is so important, but rather the sense which the flame is communicating. It's similar to the psychic bond you have with a person you are having sex with – things are understood directly.

It is harder to interpret the flames if you have a lot of expectation invested in the matter you are praying or casting a spell for, since if the outcome is super-important to you, the tendency is to engage in wishful thinking – to read the flame the way you want to read it – rather than to feel directly what the flame is saying. On the contrary, you have to let go of your own expectations and be open to whatever is happening. That's all, it's not difficult.

If you don't feel comfortable with all the ritual, you can dispense with it. The ritual is just for your own sake, to lend a sense of importance and ceremony to the occasion – not to impress the Spirit. The only things of importance are to cast your spell with true longing, at a propitious time.

When you finish casting the spell, leave the area and let the incense and candle burn down. Then dismantle the altar and dispose of what's left of the candle and incense by burying them. Once a spell has been cast there's no need to repeat it unless you feel your own resolve weakening and want to strengthen it. Be assured that spells carried out in good faith always work, so don't waste them on anything frivolous, since then you're committed to it. Be sure you really want what you're asking for. And, pay especial attention to little things that happen to you and in your dreams in the hours and days after you cast your spell.

Notes:

[1] Complete instructions on how to use Planetary Hours, with tables, appear in my book *Planetary Hours*.

VI – Science Debunked

Materialistic science,[1] like most fundamentalist religions, is extremely unreasoning and bigoted. When confronted with phenomena which don't fit its presuppositions, it closes its eyes and pretends that such phenomena don't exist. There is plenty of evidence, from all times and civilizations, that magic and astrology work, that spirits exist and can communicate with people, and so on. Indeed, about the only civilization on earth up to this time which rejects these notions is ours. "We know better now" say the scientists. How do they know this? Have they examined the subject objectively? No, they haven't done this. Even to suggest such an investigation during this dark age of rationalistic materialism would require the utmost intellectual courage and devotion to the truth. The results would bring down ultimate rejection and vituperation on one's head from the academic establishment. This is what happened to Carlos Castaneda.

Materialistic science believes that it is describing an objective, factual reality. In fact it is, like everyone else, creating its own reality. Scientists are not discovering the laws of nature; they are inventing them. The true pioneers of science – the Einsteins, Plancks, and Heisenbergs – are well aware of this fact even if the credulous hoi polloi of science are not.[2]

It is important to remember that science is a body of knowledge that has been built up over many thousands of years by many thousands of thinkers working from many different points of view and philosophical perspectives. However it has happened here and there that science has fallen into the hands of unreasoning zealots with a particular ideological axe to grind; and when that has happened science, in the sense of being an objective search for intellectual truth, winds up being a polemic to defend some political agenda. That is what occurred in Communist Russia with Lysenkoism and in Nazi Germany with "Aryan science"; and that is what has happened in capitalistic academia over the past century

What is Magic?

with the cult of materialism. The materialists with their statistical version of truth, perhaps in overreaction to the fundamentalist Christian creationist view, have completely abandoned any pretense of intellectual objectivity. As a result a non-academic version of science has developed to investigate such important matters as the thousands of reports – which tend to be quite similar in content – of after-death experiences by people who were revived; of psychic healing; of past lives; of spirit communications; etc. (not to mention astrology). What we are debunking here is not the body of knowledge which is science, but rather the smug narrow-mindedness of materialism. The materialists have such absolute power in academia and the media, and have so confused the issue with disinformation and cowed their critics with ridicule, that any criticism of materialism and its dictatorial tactics is touted as an attack on science itself.

Modern physics says, in a nutshell, that the universe is not how it appears to be to our normal, everyday perception. This is precisely what magicians and Buddhists have been saying all along. It's great that some of academic science has finally caught up to what mystics have been saying for thousands of years. However, the materialistic life sciences such as biology and psychology, not to mention neuroscience, are still back in the dark ages. They haven't yet figured out what modern physics is saying. Biology and psychology are still laboring under the old "linear time, objective space" view. Wake up, people! Materialism cannot comprehend that time and space are completely subjective (learned rules of behavior). There is NO objective reality consisting of solid, discrete objects out there; all there is, is a dream, a mass hallucination, which we have been trained to interpret with the illusion of orderliness (time and space). There's no way that what is really going on can be described by materialism except by asserting that e.g. psychic phenomena, precognition, past lives, etc. don't exist. Since practically everybody has experienced these things at one time or another for themselves, most people know where the truth lies. However everyone's afraid of being ridiculed if they have the temerity to point out publicly that the emperor is stark naked. Most people –

including many scientists who would never admit this openly for fear of reprisal – know quite well that it's materialistic science that's the lie, not magic or astrology.

We must constantly keep in mind that materialism is a religion like any other. It is an opinion which has no factual basis. It is merely a matter of faith amongst true believers, who happen to be in the majority and in absolute, dictatorial control of academia at the present time. When Georg Cantor invented set theory a century ago he was assailed by orthodox mathematicians not only because he tried to develop a calculus of infinite numbers, which was considered outside the bounds of proper scientific inquiry, but also because he invented a new type of proof which orthodox mathematicians rejected. Eventually a new generation of mathematicians came along which accepted Cantor's ideas, and now set theory is very much at the center of modern mathematical thought. The point is that what is accepted as proper science at a given time is a popularity contest pure and simple. There is nothing objective about it. And the materialistic definition of truth – statistical significance – is merely *a* definition of truth, not *the* definition of truth. Indeed, it is a rather lousy definition: statistics is not a measure of truth but rather of ignorance – an admission that you've somehow lost the thread of what's really going on.[3] Materialists throw out the baby and then fatuously scrutinize the bath water.

There is nothing to prove or disprove in magical science; there's nothing to debate. Magical science is a collection of pointers put together by more experienced practitioners to help their neophyte brethren understand what they are experiencing and where they are going, which is why magical and astrological texts written hundreds or thousands of years ago still speak to us today. Magical science makes no pretense of describing reality because 1) there is no "reality" and 2) all descriptions (thought forms, concepts, belief systems) are false.[4]

As long as you only look at this one little piece of the universe over here – things moving at slow speeds – then the old, Newtonian description works pretty well. But when you look at things moving near the speed of light, you need a new,

What is Magic?

Einsteinian, description to fit the observed facts. Similarly, when you look at this little piece of the universe over there – that which can be apprehended with the mind – then materialistic science works pretty well. But when you look at that which can only be apprehended with intuition; with feelings; by direct knowing; then materialistic science fails miserably. Materialists get around this by saying that there is no way to quantify feelings and intuition – subjective experience, *qualia* – and therefore these are not a proper subject for scientific inquiry; *as if there is any other sort of experience besides subjective experience.*

That magical science cannot be analyzed with statistics doesn't address the issue of whether magic is true. It is merely a commentary on the limitations of the materialistic approach to scientific inquiry. Magical events are too unique and ephemeral to be measured in a materialistic way because they are not mental abstracts but rather feelings. Take omens, for example, which have meaning only to the person for whom the Spirit is manifesting but not for anyone else who might be present. This doesn't mean that omens don't exist or are merely a figment of one person's imagination. Rather, it means that statistical analysis – the current criterion of scientific truth – is too crude an instrument to encompass or measure magical phenomena.

Statistical significance is no more a measure of truth than biblical authority is a measure of truth. Both statistics and the Bible merely represent different opinions as to where truth is to be found. Magicians reject both of these definitions of truth. (However consensual validation – two or more people witnessing the same event and agreeing on what they witnessed – is obtainable even with magical events when the participants have been trained – or are able from birth – to intuit such things. At Mayan ceremonies, for example, pretty much everyone present who has any sensitivity can pick up the messages which the spirits are sending. Similarly, replication of results by other researchers is as applicable to magical science as to materialistic science: that's how we learn it in the first place, and how experienced magicians train neophytes).

Laboratory statistical studies to prove or disprove "ESP" are silly. Magical science just doesn't work that way. For example, when I do rituals to invoke spirits, sometimes I feel the spirits' presence and sometimes I don't. You can't go into magic making arrogant demands; you can only humbly invite, which is why statistical studies of psychic phenomena will always come up empty.

If psychic phenomena, which are commonly experienced and have been reported by many people throughout human history cannot be measured statistically, then the obvious conclusion is that *statistics are irrelevant* to what is actually going on. The cult of materialism which has captured and imprisoned science has particularly corrupted those fields, such as psychology and anthropology, which would otherwise be most helpful in understanding what psychic phenomena (altered states of consciousness) really are, and by contrast what everyday life (an unaltered state of consciousness) really is.

The absurdity of the materialist position is illustrated by the ongoing argument in biology over whether animals possess consciousness. This sort of shameless arrogance makes one wonder whether sociobiologists possess consciousness.[5] It's precisely the same as the Nazi theories of superior race; and it's used to justify the same sort of cruelty and butchery.

Magical science is a science in the exact same sense of the word as materialistic science. However, the reality it describes and the techniques it uses are quite different from those of the materialists. For example, there is no genetic mechanism involved in fetal development. The materialists get off the track when they suppose there to be some sort of pre-programmed blueprint which nature follows blindly. Materialism considers the development of the embryo in the womb to be an automatic, mechanical process, when in fact it is better characterized as a learning process. The mother actively shapes the child in her womb by her feelings, attitudes, beliefs, etc. no less than she does after the child is born. The reason why Negro children are born to Negro parents and Caucasian children are born to Caucasian parents is precisely the same reason why American children speak

What is Magic?

English and Chinese children speak Chinese – i.e. because they have learned to do these things from their parents. A Negro mother "teaches" her unborn infant to be a Negro, just as later she will teach him to speak English. The geneticists' explanation of why Negro parents have Negro children is like the Greek myths' explanations of natural phenomena that they didn't understand.

The magician's worldview is no more true nor false than the materialistic, Christian, Islamic, etc. worldviews. You create your own reality. All worldviews are false because they are not and can never be true. What is really going on out there in the universe cannot in any way be comprehended by mind and its intellectual constructs (thought forms). As Hans Hahn said, "Our thinking consists of tautological transformation; it is incapable of comprehending a reality." Reality can only be apprehended with feeling, by direct knowing. The reason why we adopt the magicians' belief system, knowing that it is false, is to set up a counterpoint or contradiction with everyday society's worldview. This gives us a means of detaching from both worldviews, from intellection, altogether. Then feeling – intent – takes over.

There is no rational reason why the universe is the way it is. The idea that e.g. competition for scarce resources is the driving force behind evolution is the obvious conclusion that a capitalist would come to; just as the idea that things are the way they are because that is God's will is the only explanation that a Jew, Christian, or Muslim needs. But to a magician there is no reason for anything: things are the way they are as the result of completely random processes, and seeing any kind of order in how things are is narcissistic, *post hoc*, wishful thinking.[6]

Elephants don't have long proboscises because this confers an evolutionary advantage. Rather, they just have them, period. Any evolutionary advantage this bestows is a post hoc, materialistic interpretation: things are the way they are because that's how they are, and this explains why they are that way. Anyone who discerns any purpose in the outworkings of the universe – whether this purpose is conceived of as the will of God, or survival of the fittest and most prolific reproducers, or the selfishness of genes – is looking at things backwards. Both Christianity and rationalistic materialism are projecting images which aren't there. Like the cabalistic Gematria which finds hidden connections in every biblical name and phrase, or like a paranoid who detects sinister plots against him in every chance occurrence, Christianity and materialism project meaning and purpose onto complete chaos. There is no purpose to anything except as in retrospect it can be argued that things are the way they are because that is how they were meant to be. But this is an illusion, the *post hoc ergo propter hoc* fallacy, which in turn is predicated on the fallacy of linear time.

Actually, magic has a much better grip on what is really going on out there (in terms of which is the cause and which is the effect) than materialism does; so for *us* to follow *them* is completely asinine. The world is *not* a mechanism; to describe it in mechanistic terms it is necessary to ignore about 99% of what is actually going on, and to pretend that the 1% you've got left is all there is.

This is not to say that there is no causality in the universe: effects do not arise without a cause. However that causality is not embedded in linear time, and indeed it is too complex to analyze rationally (though here and there its results can be anticipated or predicted by intuition / feeling, as we do in astrology). What most of us take to be causality is merely an illusion – mistaking how humans in our society make agreements amongst themselves for laws of the universe; as if golf or the latest Paris fashions were somehow universal principles with application outside of human society. What we take to be causality is merely *post hoc* sophistry: "See, I told you so!" But it doesn't prove anything whatsoever. There is no reason for anything. *There is no reason, period*. The only thing which exists in the universe is feelings, which we have termed "intent". And these cannot be apprehended by mind.

The present race in cognitive science to solve the mystery of consciousness is never going to be won by materialism. As long as you are looking south, you'll never see the pole star; and as long as you are looking outside

What is Magic? 71

yourself you'll never understand what consciousness is. Concepts are not an adequate tool for understanding consciousness. Only materialistic hubris would believe that. We have gone as far as we can with concepts. The philosophy of materialism – very much like the philosophy of fundamentalist Christian creationism – refuses to acknowledge this fact: that its tools are outmoded and new ones (namely intent: direct knowing as opposed to knowledge that can be communicated verbally) must be employed to proceed further. Just as slavish, mindless adherence to Aristotelian and Christian tradition retarded the progress of science for centuries, so too is the false doctrine of materialism retarding the progress of science at the present time.

Materialistic platforms such as the *Skeptic* magazines and the websites which "objectively" criticize astrology are star chambers.[7] Like the Inquisition which forced Galileo to recant what he knew was the truth, materialistic scientists decry the truth of subjectivism. Materialistic scientists, like the Catholic church of old, have a vested interest in keeping their own teachings predominant. Anyone who dares to contradict these teachings is pilloried just as Galileo was. Carlos Castaneda, for example, who has brought us the most important new information of the past few millennia, was smeared, vilified, and drummed out of academia.

Look at the diatribe against astrology a few years ago by 186 famous scientists, none of whom bothered investigating astrology before denouncing it! Thirty years ago French researcher Michel Gauquelin proved the existence of an astrological effect statistically, and his results have been replicated independently by other researchers. He did what these guys say they want: he proved the existence of an astrological effect according to the statistical canons of materialistic truth.[8] Yet materialistic scientists *still* reject astrology. What does this say about scientists' pretensions to being champions of truth? Indeed, the materialistic model is a classic case of bad science: discarding any information which contradicts its preconceived assumptions.

Anthropology, economics, and psychology are (or better said: should be) the quintessential sciences because they make no pretense to studying anything beyond human nature. However all science is merely the study of human nature; or of human cognition, if you will; or of modern human cognition would be better said, since ancient humans' cognitive processes were very, very different from ours.

All that science studies is the way that humans make sense of the world. All materialistic scientists are doing is peering into a mirror and calling that the universe. Science is not the study of an objective reality, because there is *no* objective reality. Just because two humans can get together and agree that a ball, for example, is red and round and a foot in diameter doesn't really say anything about that ball. Rather, it is a description of how humans in our society make agreements amongst themselves.

This is a very difficult point to grasp, or to agree with, even if grasped. This is because you have been so indoctrinated with the assumption that you are a separated perceiver of an outside reality. Look at it like this: two Communists reading the same political news item in the newspaper will usually come to the same conclusions about it even if they can't confer on it beforehand. They already agree about the nature of their reality: they see everything in terms of class struggle, rich exploiting poor, and capital and labor continually at odds. Therefore anything that happens they will fit into that worldview, and they will agree on what really happened in that news story. Similarly, two capitalists reading the same news story will agree with each other on what actually happened in that news item. However, their view of the occurrence will probably be very much at odds with the interpretation of the Communists. In the same way, materialistic scientists confronted with objective phenomena try to fit them into their pre-conceived worldview, which a priori excludes astrology and magic.

I believe that most people know in their hearts that materialistic science is shamelessly lying when it denies the truth of magic. Of course, magical science cannot be proven true by materialistic canons of truth any more than Galileo could prove the validity of Copernican theory by appealing to the Bible, as the Inquisitionists of that time demanded. For

What is Magic?

one thing, materialistic science is based upon completely different presuppositions than magical science, such as linear time,[9] duality, the existence of an objective reality, and that statistics measure truth. Materialistic scientists and magicians are not looking at the same phenomena. Or rather, they are, but from irreconcilably contradictory points of view; or better said, from different taken-for-granted cognitive assumptions. The materialist looks outward for answers, whereas the magician looks inward. But I believe that in the next century conventional science will evolve to include what is now considered magic. Then it won't be considered magic at all. Modern science is in fact magic, but its practitioners don't call it that or understand it in those terms because they are blinded by the tenets of their fundamentalist religion, the chief one being that the world is mechanistic rather than *alive*. That it's something we can stomp on with impunity and it will never stomp back.

The ideal of materialistic science is a hell world, and that's where they're taking us. In societies where they have a modicum of respect for life they don't do vivisection or Auschwitz-type medical experiments, so they don't learn all the neat things you can learn by cold-bloodedly destroying other beings. Materialism is basically a form of black magic (except it is far more stupid and inept than real black magic).

It's not only the animal and human sacrifices that present-day scientists are involved in that mirror disrespect. Just the way astronomers look at the stars, with no ability to feel what they are seeing, is disrespectful. Probably most astronomers were originally drawn to astronomy by a sense of awe, but the disrespect which is part and parcel of materialism soon confuses young astronomers. And God help them if they avow before their inquisitional fellows an intuitive acceptance of the veracity of astrology or magic!

The materialists' argument – like their capitalist masters' argument – is that "it works." But so does a scorched earth policy against Mayan Indians work to isolate guerrillas. And so did the bombing of Hiroshima work: undoubtedly that saved many lives on both sides. But the underlying assumption in both cases is mistaken. It doesn't lead to happiness or joy.

Shameless cruelty works really well; but it makes for a hell world. Shameless arrogance and contempt are an intrinsic component of materialism in all of its forms (standing above and subduing nature – and other people – instead of approaching them humbly and respectfully). Besides, capitalism and materialism don't "work". At this point in history it is very clear exactly how well capitalism and materialism are "working", and exactly where these stupid, destructive mindsets are leading us.

Science doesn't have to be so cruel and heartless. You don't have to rape the universe for knowledge. You can ask it nicely what you want to know. Luther Burbank produced many new varieties of plants by talking to them. According to Rudolf Steiner, that is how all the fruit crops which people now use were originally developed from wild plants. Ancient Mesoamerican magicians created maize from the native grass *teosinte* thousands of years ago in a manner which thoroughly baffles modern botanists, since the genetic manipulation techniques required for this transmutation have only existed for the last twenty years.

By choosing materialistic science in its current, heartless manifestation we are foregoing the experience of the world as joyous. Rationalism doesn't have to be divorced from magic, which is as much a science as physics or biology. Magical science just operates on different assumptions. Actually it is a different cognitive system altogether. Indeed, Sir Isaac Newton – the founder of modern science – was a magician. In John Maynard Keynes' words, "Newton was not the first of the age of reason. He was the last of the magicians, the last of the Babylonians and Sumerians." The majority of Newton's writings have been suppressed by the materialistic Inquisition because they dealt with magic and alchemy.[10]

Materialistic science was well suited to agricultural and industrial human society. It led to a great deal of material progress. But there are too many people now; and they're messing the earth up. That sort of crabbed, niggling, arrogant, and shameless mindset won't work anymore. Materialistic science has perverted the quest for intellectual truth and embraced a smug, shallow sophistry in its stead. What the

What is Magic?

human race desperately needs, and is now ready for, is a new worldview, based upon broader principles of intellectual truth than any which materialistic science can ever encompass. The human race is on the brink of a scientific revolution greater than the one which rocked the 16th and 17th centuries. We have to start – or restart, since these were our guiding lights when humans were still hunter / gatherers – setting aside all our intellection, our opinions and beliefs, and opening our hearts to what the earth is trying to tell us.

One nice thing about magical science is that it really doesn't matter whether it is true or not. It's the best bet. Materialistic religion assumes that everything's all screwed up, but someday science will figure it all out. Magic, by contrast, assumes nothing. If you are going to be saved, it will be by your own efforts; by being wide awake instead of pulling woolly assumptions over your eyes to lull yourself into a stupor. You must take 100% responsibility for your own salvation.

Magicians believe that the God Materialism is leading us to hell in a handbasket. Three Mile Island and Chernobyl are good examples (n.b., this was written before Fukushima) – loud and clear warnings to anyone who's not asleep – and yet they're still building them. It is true that materialistic science and technology have brought many people a high level of comfort and convenience, but at the cost of bankrupting their spirit and joy. Are you happy in your work, your relationships, your life? Do you know anyone who is?

Magic and astrology were the world religion once, and they shall be the world religion again, because people have had enough of the emptiness, meaninglessness, and short-sighted stupidity of materialism. *E pur si muove!*

Notes:

[1] By the term "materialism" is meant the belief that, in the words of cognitive philosopher Daniel Dennett, "there is only one sort of stuff, namely *matter* – the physical stuff of physics, chemistry, and physiology – and the mind is somehow nothing but a physical phenomenon. In short, the

mind is the brain." – Dennett, Daniel *Consciousness Explained*, Penguin 1991 p. 33.

The science of magic, by contrast, takes the Idealistic view that the physical world, including the physical body and brain, are merely projections of the mind; in exactly the same way that the world of dreams and the body we have while we are dreaming are projections of the mind. Being awake is merely a more highly evolved form of dreaming, and it is only our belief that what is happening to us is real that makes it seem real (whether we are awake or dreaming).

[2] "Philosophically ... the implications of quantum mechanics are psychedelic. Not only do we influence our reality, but in some degree we actually create it. ... Metaphysically, this is very close to saying that we create certain properties because we choose to measure those properties." - Zukav, Gary, *The Dancing Wu Li Masters*, Bantam NYC 1980, page 28. See also *Spooked* by Adam Gopnik, New Yorker magazine 11/30/2015 page 84, http://archives.newyorker.com/?i=2015-11-30#folio=84.

[3] Statistics are not a measure of truth but rather a way of obfuscating truth. The best proof of this is that astrological and magical phenomena cannot be measured statistically. For example, according to materialist theory, buying numerous lottery tickets increases your chances of winning the lottery. But according to magical theory, buying more than one lottery ticket actually decreases your chances of winning, since it demonstrates lack of faith – trying to second-guess or fake out the Spirit.

Materialist critics of well-documented cases of past life memories or the commonality of near death experiences dismiss this evidence as "anecdotal"; as if statistics was something other than a bunch of materialists telling each other anecdotes. The decision about what to measure or not measure is completely SUBJECTIVE; and the decision about how to skew the statistical results to obtain the outcome which one's capitalist masters (who are funding the research) desire is also completely SUBJECTIVE. Statistics is a valid system

What is Magic?

of measurement as long as you confine it to flipping coins or computing odds for poker or bridge hands; but when you try to apply it to the "real world", you're talking trash. Indeed, reading materialists' criticisms of each other's work is a most illuminating excursus into just how phony and meaningless the whole statistical approach is, since it can be (and in fact is) bent any way you want to prove anything you want. Even the materialists themselves are beginning to suspect that the statistical definition of truth is false (see *The Truth Wears Off* by Jonah Lehrer, *The New Yorker Magazine* December 13, 2010, Page 52 posted at: http://www.newyorker.com/reporting/2010/12/13/101213fa_fact_lehrer).

4   There is only one canonical way of doing biology or physics; but there are lots of ways of doing astrology or magic; and they all work. For example, Franz Bardon's conception of spirits and how to invoke them (*The Practice of Magical Evocation*) is quite different from mine. Similarly, Carlos Castaneda's conception of demons (*The Active Side of Infinity*) is different from mine. This doesn't mean that one is right and the other is wrong. We are all sharing our personal experiences, which are necessarily diverse. Once you step outside of the bounds of everyday society with its consensual agreements, you no longer have any guidelines or guiderails to hang onto except for what your spirits tell you; and also the wisdom gleaned from your own experience. This is why it is useful for the magical tyro to read different authors, or to work with different teachers, to get different takes on the subject.

5   Of course this depends upon how you choose to define "consciousness". Magical science is Panpsychist in that it considers that any being who can feel feelings possesses consciousness. Thus everything that lives – animals, plants, bacteria; even so-called inanimate objects such as our possessions, rocks, even mountains (especially mountains!) and caves possess consciousness.

6   Even the materialist biologists themselves are beginning to suspect that Darwin's theory of evolution is false

– projecting images which simply aren't there to find causes where there are no causes (see *What Darwin Got Wrong*, by Jerry Fodor and Massimo Piattelli-Palmarini, Farrar, Strauss, Giroux 2009).

[7] Although the materialists are quite correct that tests to prove the competence of astrologers are usually embarrassing failures, the fault, Dear Brutus, lies not in astrology but in the stigma which the materialists have heaped upon astrology, so that very few first-rate minds are attracted to the field. Part of the problem, too, is that the materialists demand an impossible standard of accuracy which astrology, because of its very nature, is incapable of providing. The universe is not as mechanistic as the materialists would like to believe; rather, it is a matter of free will and of possible outcomes. Astrology cannot predict that e.g. "at 12:37 pm on August 3rd you will slip on ice and break your left arm above the elbow." Psychics – and psychic astrologers – can sometimes do this; but they use intuition to do it, not astrology. To demand pinpoint accuracy from astrology qua astrology is unreasonable and silly; although once in a while you can do it.

[8] see Dean, Geoffrey, *Recent Advances in Natal Astrology*, Astrological Association (Australia) 1977, page 380 ff for details.

[9] Where materialistic science sees time as linear, magic sees time as rhythmic. Materialistic science measures points and intervals along a well-ordered continuum, whereas magical science measures cycles upon cycles. This is what astrology is all about: the moment of birth can be viewed as a point along a linear continuum, as it is in rationalistic materialism; or, conversely, it can be viewed as a stage in the unfoldment of potentialities on various levels – i.e. as the intersection of many different interpenetrating cycles, as it is in astrology.

Time is *not* linear. Everything that has ever happened, and ever will happen, in all lifetimes and realities, is all going on at once, in an eternal NOW moment. It is more accurate to describe time as an emanation of birth – death – rebirth; and

What is Magic?

what we see as linear time is but a fragmentary way of apprehending this phenomenon which has evolved in tandem with human society. Linear time is a completely human invention, like golf or the latest Paris fashions; a set of rules which have no reference to anything outside of human experience (animals have a relatively undeveloped sense of linear time compared to humans – i.e. are more centered in the now moment, don't apprehend so much of a past and future as humans do). Linear time is predicated on linear thinking. When thinking stops – when the constant internal dialogue which most people engage in from the minute they awaken to the minute they go to sleep ceases – then so too does linear time.

[10] Keynes, John Maynard, *Newton, the Man*; from Newman, James, *The World of Mathematics*, Simon & Schuster NYC 1956 pages 277, 282: "A large section (of Newton's papers), judging by the handwriting amongst the earliest, relates to alchemy – transmutation, the philosopher's stone, the elixir of life. The scope and character of these papers have been hushed up, or at least minimized, by nearly all those who have inspected them."

VII – Demons

The information given in this book about demons, curses, and black magicians is not theoretical, armchair speculation. It's truth that I was forced to acknowledge at a certain point in my life when I found myself eyeball-to-eyeball with demons during an all-out battle with a black witch. I didn't believe in demons or curses before this experience even though I had been channeling spirit guides and nature spirits for some years prior. Therefore I certainly don't blame anyone else for not believing in these things. Unfortunately, they're true.

In our society the stigma attached to believing in demons is quite strong. Anyone who admits to believing in demons is considered crazy or stupid, or perhaps evil, and is no longer taken seriously. Demons do exist, however; and becoming a magician requires facing up to this truth and dealing with it, not sweeping it under the rug. Magicians have to deal with how things really are and not worry about what other people might think or say about them. To a magician, the problem of demons is the most pressing issue facing the human race; and our addressing, or failing to address, this issue will decide our future, or lack of future, as a species (for another take on the issue of demons, see the "Mud Shadows" chapter of Carlos Castaneda's *The Active Side of Infinity*[1]).

The trouble with all of the false stereotypes of black magic and demons in the popular media (particularly that these things don't exist) is that they prevent us from understanding what is really going on. As many fundamentalist Christians rightly believe, demons are everywhere. In fact, they run the whole shebang. When we talk about demons, we're not talking about Transylvania: we're talking about trouble right here in River City. Demons are pretty much all over the place, and they run our society. The government, media, academia, churches (especially the churches!) are of the demons, by the demons, and for the demons. The movie *The Matrix* is actually a pretty good picture of what our society is really like, but with

What is Magic?

demons rather than machines behind the scenes pulling the strings. Like germs, demons are everywhere. Therefore, they are not something to be frightened of or worried about. In fact, the people who are the most freaked out by demons, such as Inquisitors and witch hunters, are usually the most demon-possessed themselves. Likewise, the people who are the most uptight about black magic are usually the ones who are doing the most black magic themselves. Most demon-possessed people, like most black magicians, consider themselves to be upstanding, righteous, pious citizens.

Demons are blandishing everybody – even those not specifically possessed – all the time. Most of your thoughts of how marvelous and wonderful you are; and how misunderstood you are; and how the people who don't appreciate you will be sorry some day; as well as most of your sexual and glory fantasies – not to mention angry and fearful thoughts – are just demons directing your thinking. Those kinds of thoughts aren't "your" thoughts at all. They are just thoughts which demons implant in your mind.

However many, if not most, of the people in our society – including practically all of our leaders in all areas – are out-and-out demon-possessed. That's how they got to be so successful in what is basically a demonic society. Indeed, it's quite possible that you may be demon-possessed. I was possessed for the first 40 years of my life, until my spirit guides pointed that fact out to me and explained to me how to cast them out. It's no big deal, really, either to be possessed or to cast demons out. This will be explained later.

Here's a fictional example which illustrates how people unconsciously call demons in to possess them in moments of great self-pity, taken from John O'Hara's novel *Appointment in Samarra*. Notice how Julian English's wife calls in a demon of her own in response to Julian's demon:

"He did. What's the use of trying to fool myself? I know he did. I know he did and no matter what excuses I make or how much I try to tell myself that he didn't, I'll only come back to the same thing: He did. I know he did. And what for? For a dirty little thrill with a woman who – oh, I thought he'd got all that out of his system. Didn't he have enough of that before he

married me? ... Ah, Julian, you stupid, hateful, mean, low, contemptible little son of a bitch that I hate! You do this to me, and know that you do this to me! Know it! Did it on purpose! ... You big charmer, you. You irresistible great big boy, turning on the charm like the water in the tub; turning on the charm like the water in the tub; turning on the charm turning on the charr-arm, turning on the charm like the water in the tub. I hope you die.

"I hope you die because you have killed something fine in me, suh. Ah hope you die. Yes-suh, Ah hope you die. You have killed something mighty fine in me, English, old boy, old kid, old boy. What Ah mean is, did you kill something fine in me or did you kill something fine."[2]

This example is a good illustration of the way in which people call in demons to possess them when they feel especially vulnerable and in need of drastic protection. In most cases the appeal to demons is unconscious. Once demons are called in to possess a person, whether consciously or not, they don't leave unless they are deliberately exorcised.

What are demons like? They're like humans, but far more intelligent and cunning, and also sleazier. If you've ever met a psychopath face-to-face, then you know the type; but more so. Totally self-centered and sleazy. Demons are also really touchy, uptight, and self-important. They hate being ignored, and absolutely freak out at being laughed at. The demons which I have met face-to-face, in dreaming, appeared like normal people, but there was something very slimy about them. That is how I knew who they were.

Most of my encounters with demons were oblique. I could feel their presence because I would start getting angry for no reason. This is because I'm an angry person: a fearful person they would make fearful, a lustful person they would make lustful, and so on. Demons survive by generating and feeding off of your self-pity. They feed thoughts into your mind; then when you react by releasing desire lines in response, the demons snap them up. Demons are basically everywhere. For example, when you are driving and another driver cuts in right ahead of you and you beep the horn in anger, that's in fact an exchange between that guy's demons and your own.

Some psychopaths such as Adolf Hitler and Pol Pot got their dazzling, hypnotizing charm from the demons which possessed them. Other psychopaths like Joseph Stalin and Saddam Hussein were bestial thugs. What demons often give their hosts is an extraordinary cunning and a feel for the jugular. They sense precisely how far they can go and what they can get away with; and they have no scruples whatsoever about destroying anyone or anything that gets in their way.

Not all demon-possessed people become world leaders, of course, and not all are psychopathic. Many people who are depressed, repressed, angry and irritable all the time, constantly ill, addicted to drugs or sex or whatever, self-destructive generally, are possessed by demons. You can stand in a supermarket and watch the demon-possessed people go by: the harried mother pulling her kid in tow as she shops, yelling at the kid and yanking his arm out of its socket to drag him away from the things which normal curiosity leads him to explore; the old geezer with a perpetual scowl, pushing his shopping cart aggressively with an "out of my way, buddy!" snarl on his face; the care-worn, overburdened, downtrodden people dragging their weary selves up and down the aisles.

It's not too hard to tell if people are demon-possessed when they get old. When they are still young, there's usually enough of the original person left there so that you can't see the demons as readily (except in certain revealing moments now and then). As the people get older, however, the demons eat up more and more of their souls and their joy. If, as people age, they get lighter and more joyous, then they're not demon-possessed. On the other hand if they get more uptight, nastier, depressed, or more self-pitying as they age, then they probably are demon-possessed. This is why it's so hard to deal with those old people – you're not dealing with the person anymore, just with a demon who subsists by sucking other people's energy (having burned out most of its host's energy).

Demons are not evil. They're doing what they have to do in order to eat, just like the rest of us. There is no evil per se in the universe. If you want to call the necessity of killing and devouring other beings in order to survive evil, then the one you've got to blame for this is the One who made that rule in the first place. That was not Satan. Demons have to eat just like everybody else. What demons eat is what we call feelings, especially uptight feelings. Demons survive by generating and feeding off of our self-pity. To demons, we humans are self-pity machines programmed by them to produce the most delectable demon delicacies with our constant moaning and groaning, and our thinking we're so great.

Demons are actually not that difficult to deal with – at least as compared with humans. Although they are incredibly intelligent and cunning, if you don't harbor evil intentions in your heart they won't bother you. Unlike humans, demons obey certain rules; they are consistent; they won't do anything against their own best interests. Humans, on the other hand, are grossly stupid, erratic, and self-destructive. Frankly, I much, much prefer to confront demons than to have to deal with the machinations of humans.

What makes being a demon, or messing around with demons, evil is that there's no real joy or happiness in it. The way they feed themselves, and the way we feed ourselves under their influence, is uptight and ugly. It's a big rush of self-importance, and then lots of pain. Then another big rush of self-importance, and then lots of pain. It's a spiral of self-importance and pain. It's not very peaceful or pleasant. But it can't properly be characterized as evil per se. It's an extremely popular lifestyle for humans as well as demons. It's called society.

Prior to the invention of agriculture after the last ice age, about 12,000 years ago, humans were more or less like any other apes. They were more intelligent than most other animals, but not particularly smart. My guides have told me that if you could meet one of your ancestors from that period, you would consider it an animal. There's no level upon which we modern humans would consider those ancestors to be what we consider to be human.

It was an alliance that the human race forged with the race of demons during the Late Upper Paleolithic – early

What is Magic?

Neolithic era that made us the thinking, rational animals we are today. It was at that time that trapping, fishing, and hunting with dogs were invented – ensnaring game instead of hunting it directly. Then agriculture was invented – raising animals and plants instead of gathering them directly. Demons channeled new technologies to the human race through individuals who were inventors and innovators. They still do.

These indirect techniques for getting food necessitated a greater sense of planning for the future than direct hunting / gathering had required. The new social order demanded a new type of consciousness: perception and cognition tied to linear time. Planning for the future is what creates the future. Until the demons taught us about the future, all human beings had to work with was the now moment.

Linear time is the matrix of our separated, lower self. Our human ancestors, like infants, didn't have anywhere near as much sense of separatedness as we do. They were not as individuated as we are today. They lived in a more timeless frame of mind, a sense of belonging to the universe. Their mental process wasn't a matter of constant thinking, but rather of direct knowing what their ancestors, spirits, and the earth were telling them. They felt themselves to be part of an ongoing, natural process in the same way that we feel ourselves to be part of our society. Because they were not as separated as people are today, they felt less *Angst* than we do, because they had no future to worry about.

If the future didn't exist, would you care about it? It's precisely your caring and worrying about the future that conjures up its existence. You care about the future, it's important to you, whether it's winning the lottery, finding your true soul-mate, becoming famous, or going to heaven when you die. These sorts of expectations are what trap you into striving towards a future which never arrives. The other side of that coin is your past, the things that you are ashamed of and are trying to forget about (and would never reveal to another person). Everyone in our society is taught to hate themselves, and then to hide that self-hatred away. This striving towards a future and slinking away from a past is what creates the illusion that there is such a thing as a future and a past. When striving ends, so too does linear time. Another way of saying this is: our sense of linear time is the product of our linear thinking. If we stop thinking so much about the future and past and return our attention to the now moment, like ancient humans did and infants do, then the past and future lose much of their meaning. They are just not as important, so they are not as there; things are too *now*.

Our higher selves are timeless. Higher self is eternal: it is your touch with the Spirit. Higher self has to be squelched down into the straitjacket of linear time in order to create your uptight, niggling little lower self. We learned how to create a sense of linear time – a separated, lower self which is caught in a loop of constant self-reflection – of seeking glory in the future and hiding shame from the past – from our demon masters. Over the past millennia the demons have taught us everything that we modern humans now consider "human". That is to say, our civilization – all of our thinking – is demonic in origin. The qualities that we modern humans believe elevate us above the realm of animals are essentially demonic qualities. Demons taught us how to think because thinking requires concentrated effort. This effort, or being uptight – hiding shame from the past and seeking glory in the future – allows demons to suck human energy.

Generally speaking, *any* thinking about the past or future (regrets or worries as opposed to e.g. problem-solving, which is centered in the now moment) is neurotic and allows demons to suck our energy. A lot of what people consider "living with a positive mental attitude" is phony – just being in denial.

This is why adults are usually more uptight than little children, who aren't yet in a mode of constant thinking. Adults are completely accustomed to thinking every second all day long. We don't realize how much energy it takes to maintain this inner dialogue. This constant thinking, particularly when it's worried, or angry, or jealous thinking, provides fodder for the demons who surround us.

In other words, the invention of agriculture wasn't so much a matter of humans beginning to farm plants and animals for food as it was demons beginning to farm humans for food. Now, after millennia of inbreeding us, the demons

What is Magic?

have us right where they want us. Earlier generations of humans were hardy, robust, and self-reliant, which is hard fare for demons to digest. We moderns with our undisciplined, self-indulgent, decadent lifestyles have become a toothsome delight for the demons who suck us. We are fat and complacent, with no minds or wills of our own. We obediently and unquestioningly believe all the lies our government, churches, media, and so-called "science" tell us.

Our demon masters, who were overjoyed when humans invented agriculture and became a semblance of them, are presently ecstatic that humans have adopted an urban society wholly disconnected from nature. We are turning the green, loving earth into a hell world. At least when most humans were doing agriculture they were still attached to the earth's love and the rhythms of the universe. Now, urban society has cut humans off completely from the earth's love. When does anyone even look at a tree anymore except through a speeding windshield or a television screen? And the food – the Soylent Green – which people today eat from supermarkets ... Welcome to hell, folks! You don't have to wait until you die. Hell is right here, right now. The worst part of it is that most people have been trained to call this heaven. And the demons are eating it up. Eating us up.

There was nothing wrong with humans having associated with demons for the past few millennia. We learned a lot from them. We learned how to think, for starters. Now it's time we went our own way and followed our own star, because continuing to serve our demon masters will just lead to our own destruction as a species. When humans allied themselves with demons they made some sort of very unpleasant denouement inevitable; and it is our generation and our kids' generation which will have to learn how to extricate ourselves from the rubble. A magician must remain undaunted even when single-handedly confronting all of the demons in the universe, **because you are**.

I've cast demons out of people and also out of buildings they were inhabiting. I don't like doing this, though, because it scares me. When the demons are cut loose they dive into the nearest host they can grab onto. The time I cast demons out of a building where black magicians had lived previously, I followed my spirits' advice and lit a censer with copal incense. Then I circled the building repeating an appeal to the demons to leave: "You are not wanted here anymore, you'll be a lot happier in another place where you are more appreciated. In the name of the nine Mayan gods (my patron spirits) I cast you out!" I tried to muster confidence which I didn't actually feel for the "I cast you out!" part. Then at each corner of the building I set off a chain of firecrackers, since demons have highly refined sensibilities and dislike clamor. After the firecrackers went off at the first corner I could sense something coming loose. By the last corner I sensed they were completely loose.

I then left, but as I walked away I started talking nervously to my assistant about the ritual we had just performed, "Hey, that really worked, didn't it?" At that instant I sensed something diving into me, which really freaked me out. I started jumping up and down to shake whatever it was out of me, and at the same time I forced myself to think about something else, to blank my mind. Ever since then I try to avoid casting out demons. When it is absolutely unavoidable I do it in a place where I am protected, a nearby cave which is a Mayan holy place. I certainly don't advise casting demons out of other people unless you've got spirit helpers in whom you have the utmost faith, such as Jesus, Krishna, or Buddha, backing you up.

I'm of the opinion that people should cast out their own demons. They called them in, and they should take the responsibility for casting them out themselves. The exception to this would be in the cases of children or people who are too crazy to do it for themselves.

Sometimes people ask me, "I think my parent (or spouse or loved one) might be demon-possessed. Is there anything I can do to cast it out?" My usual answer is negative. Demons won't leave if the host doesn't want them to leave, or they'll immediately return if cast out. In our society most people don't even believe in the existence of demons, much less seriously entertain the possibility that they themselves could

What is Magic?

be possessed. Demon-possessed people are always right and the other fellow is always wrong – that's their hallmark. Moreover, most people, especially old people, have become comfortable with their demons. They're afraid to have to start living their own lives and making their own decisions again. It's easier just to be uptight and miserable – it is even seen as a badge of honor to be a grumpy old person. Bit-by-bit they surrender all their joy to their demons, until in the end the demons are all that's left.

I once counseled a friend of mine who was in an extremely dysfunctional marriage, "I think you're demon-possessed. Even though I know you don't believe in demons, just for the hell of it why don't you go to the holy Mayan cave, light a candle, and ask the spirit of the place 'If, on the off chance, I am indeed possessed by demons, please cast them out.'" She did this and reported later that the moment she said those words her candle flickered even though there was no wind, and a pain – like an ice pick – shot through her head. What happened next in her life was that she split up with her husband. My interpretation of this is that without the demon's protection she was too vulnerable to handle the Punch and Judy show she was involved in, so she terminated the relationship. Just casting out demons that may be possessing you doesn't automatically make you any happier. It just makes it possible for you to become happier. But there's no way to get even to square one until you clear the demons out of the way.

Luckily it's pretty easy to cast demons out of yourself. All that's required is the desire to do so, and the firm decision to get rid of them. If you are suffering from a chronic or incurable disease, or are battling against some form of addiction, then casting out demons is the first step in self-healing. It's the first step in self-healing for most of us, since so many of us are demon-possessed. Until you get rid of any demons that may be possessing you and reassert control over your own intent, all your spiritual endeavors are just whistling in the wind. Complete instructions on how to cast out demons are given in my book *Thought Forms*. To summarize:

To cast out demons, go to whatever place you are accustomed to pray at. Power spots or power trees are good places to do this, especially if you have faith in the power of the place or tree to brace your spirit. Light a candle and ask the deity to whom you usually pray that, if there happens to be a maleficent influence in your life, to please cast it out! You must make this prayer in a true spirit of decisiveness and determination. If you pray in a spirit of doubt or hesitation, the demon will use your vacillation to defeat your prayer. Mars planetary hours are good hours to take decisive, irrevocable action; to stand up for yourself; but this is merely a help, not a necessity.

Demons are always trying to convince you that you are doing everything possible to make yourself happy, but at the same time they undermine your efforts. A wishy-washy prayer to cast out a demon may make you believe that you've accomplished something, but the demon will weasel past it. Thus demons have to be cast out in a mood of unbending intent and decision. That's all that's required – unbending intent to cast the demon out. Jumping up and down and shaking your body vigorously is another way to cast them out. This is also a good way to get rid of bad moods or the bad vibes other people lay on you as well.

How will you know whether your exorcism worked? Successful exorcisms are often accompanied by sensations of something that was inside you leaving. There may be some kind of whoosh of something flying out of you and away. But this isn't always true. One way you'll know is that in the next few days you'll feel lighter, more hopeful and optimistic. Your friends will notice the difference too: they'll remark on how much better you look or feel.

Note that it sometimes happens, when someone casts out demons, that the demons return that night to terrify the person (to try to get back inside of them). If this should happen to you, just hang in there: it's only one (interminable) night of hell, and after that they'll leave you in peace. Maybe spend that first night with someone you trust to hold your hand.

If there's any doubt, though, you can always repeat the exorcism. Just make sure to do it in a mood of decisiveness and determination. That's all, it's not difficult. And, don't worry too much about this whole demon thing: if you are pure of heart, they won't bother you any.

Notes:

[1] Castaneda, Carlos, *The Active Side of Infinity*, HarperCollins NYC 1998.

[2] O'Hara, John, *Appointment in Samarra*, Bantam NYC 1966, p 176

VIII – The Nature of the Self

I'm trying not to include too much philosophy in this book. However, since the magicians' viewpoint is so different from the taken-for-granted assumptions of everyday society, some explanation of principles is necessary. There are plenty of great magicians who don't know the "why" of what they're doing. They just do it naturally and don't think about it or ask questions. But they can't explain what they do to other people, either.

The Judeo-Christian-Islamic intellectual tradition, which includes materialistic science, is a very different belief system than the magical-pagan-Buddhist tradition. The J-C-I-materialistic point of view believes that we have individual self-existence and that we live in an objective reality – a world of solid objects embedded in linear time. The magical-pagan-Buddhist view is that we do not have a personal self in spite of superficial appearances to the contrary; nor is there an objective, outside reality impinging upon us.

Most people identify their self with their physical body; and reality with the world outside their body. However, this is merely an appearance. When you are dreaming, you have a body also, and a world outside of it. That body and world seem perfectly real while you are dreaming, but when you wake up you realize that it was all just a dream.

While you are dreaming your dream body operates with all five of the usual physical senses. Therefore, you really don't have any objective criteria for deciding, at any given moment, whether you are awake or asleep. Although you can deduce whether you are awake or (lucidly) dreaming, you have no sensory basis for perceiving this distinction directly. In precisely the same way, your body when you are awake, and the world surrounding it, are just a specialized form of dreaming. You wake up from this dream when you become enlightened or die.

Something of the self must survive the death of the physical body because it's a simple matter to channel the spirits of recently deceased people. For example, when I

What is Magic?

channeled the spirits of my grandmother and mother shortly after their deaths, I was convinced that it was indeed my grandmother and mother whom I was channeling rather than e.g. some other spirits pretending to be them. This wasn't so much because they knew things that only my grandmother and mother could have known, since all spirits seem to have the capacity to read minds. Rather, I believed that it was indeed my grandmother and mother I was channeling because they cared about things that only my grandmother and mother would have cared about. My teacher, don Abel Yat, and my spiritual grandfather, don Eligio Panti, have also come to me (and their other students) on various occasions since they passed away, with information, prophecies and blessings.

In other words I can channel the spirits of the deceased, and I've taught other people to do the same thing. Funerals are a good time to do this since the spirit of the deceased usually hovers around the body for a short time after death; also it often helps to relieve people's grief to be able to converse directly with their deceased loved ones. Channeling these spirits has convinced me that there must be some sort of afterlife and some part of our self which survives death. Therefore the self must not be the same thing as the body, which ends at death.

You need not take my word for any of this. If you want to learn how to channel yourself, see my book *Magical Living* for instructions. Only fools take other people's words, ideas, and belief systems as their own without subjecting them to a rigorous personal test; and magicians are not fools.

Let us define your *higher self* to be the part that survives physical death (what W.B. Yeats referred to as "*Mask*" and what we refer to elsewhere as "true feelings" or "true purpose"); and let us define your *lower self* to be the part, including your body, which dies at physical death (what W.B. Yeats referred to as "*Will*" and what we refer to elsewhere as "importance"). You can get a clue as to what your lower self really is by observing newborns. Although newborns occupy a physical body from your point of view, that's obviously not the newborns' point of view. Newborns don't have a sense of being centered or trapped in a body. They don't even understand that they have a body. All they know is how they *feel*. If they are hungry, or in pain, they cry. However, they have no sense that it is a bodily condition which is causing their discomfort. All they know, all they are, is a feeling at a particular time.

Being in a body is an interpretation that infants learn as they grow and discover their bodies. In other words, your physical body is something that you've learned: you were not born with it. Is this cogent? It's the truth. Learning how to operate without a body – unlearning what you learned as an infant – is an important part of magicians' training.

This is what astral projection is all about: operating outside the box of the physical body. Astral projection is not so much something you learn as something you unlearn. It is a technique (or better said: a cognitive process) predicated upon the realization that the physical body has no objective existence. The physical body is an interpretation you have learned to make, and astral projection is based upon an alternative interpretation.

Consider this: a baby who is born with a severe facial deformity is considered monstrous and pitiable by the adults who see him. This image is unavoidably imposed upon the baby, who can't help but pick up this interpretation from the adults around him. Now extend the analogy one step further: when any baby is born the adults around him see him as occupying a physical body. The baby can't help but make this same interpretation.

The interpretation that you have a physical body is merely a belief, exactly like the interpretation that you have a body while you're dreaming is merely a belief. Being awake is in fact nothing more than a highly evolved and specialized form of dreaming. Waking consciousness has evolved over millions of years, since the first multi-cellular beings appeared on the earth. Therefore it has a lot of stability and momentum behind it. When you're awake, it really seems real. Your physical body really seems solid. When you bang it, it really hurts.

In fact, however, your physical body is merely a solider illusion – a more encompassing, more persistent, more

What is Magic?

convincing illusion – than the body that you have in dreams. That this physical body will die is part of the interpretation: part of the illusion that the thing had objective existence in the first place.

As adults we have a much more sharply defined and delineated sense of selfhood than infants do – by which self is meant lower self. The difference between higher self and lower self is that higher self says: "This happened", whereas lower self says: "This happened to *me*." That "me", when examined soberly and objectively, is found to consist of nothing more than self-pity in one of its numerous guises – a manifestation of either shame or glory.

You have been trained to mistakenly believe that your body is the source of your suffering; but in fact it is your suffering that is the source of your body. Your body is "made of" self-pity; that's what gives it its apparent solidity. Without self-pity when you bang it, it still hurts; but it doesn't hurt "you;" it just hurts, period. The resulting illusion of there being a solid "you" there that things are happening to, is what we call lower self.

Lower self, your self-pity, is the underlying feeling of your customary moods and concerns. Lower self consists of your nervous habits like the tensing yourself up that you feel all the time you are awake; the need to be zipping about, fidgeting and fuming, attending to this or that urgency. Lower self is the defensive wall you feel up against other people when you're having sex with them, or even just talking to them. Lower self is the attitude you put on when you wake up every morning; and the mask with which you greet life and other people all day long. If you were to wake up one day in someone else's moods and concerns, with a wholly different set of self-pity agendas, you'd feel thoroughly disoriented: you'd think you'd been jettisoned into an alien universe.

It is a big error to believe that your lower self – your self-pitying feelings such as insecurity, greed, envy, lust, jealousy – are your true feelings: that they are you (your true self). In fact, these feelings are not your feelings at all. Rather, they are your thought forms' feelings, termed *importance coverings*, which you have learned from your parents and society, and then adopted as your own.

Your self-pity – the feeling you conjure up with your customary moods and concerns – doesn't really belong to you at all. Yet that is what you have learned to identify as your "self"; and to defend with every fiber of your being. Most people are so wrapped up in their self-pity that they don't usually understand this vital point: that there is a higher self there behind the lower self. That's why you cling so hard to your self-pity: you're afraid that that is all that stands between you and annihilation. The mistake of the lower self is the assumption that *anything* stands between you and annihilation. This is a grievous tactical error. It just begs for death to come sock it to you.

In a nutshell, self-pity consists of comparing yourself to others: feeling superior or inferior to others, judging and criticizing others, and expecting things from others. That is to say, the lower self exists only in relation to other people. This is a very important point: what most people consider to be their "self" is a socialized phenomenon. Newborns do not have a lower self. They don't have a central point of reference, a sense of where they end and other begins. To newborns things are moment-to-moment, and everything is one. There's no abiding, continuing, separated "me" there.

The lower self is like a piece missing out of a jigsaw puzzle. It is wholly defined by the other people surrounding it. Magicians know that it is precisely the belief that you're better than other people that makes you no better than other people. That belief is what traps you in your lower self, and hence in your body.

Your lower self is created by your constantly thinking thoughts of shame and glory. If you analyze your constant thinking, you will realize that it consists mostly of thoughts about the past and future. Thoughts about the past evoke feelings of shame, of embarrassment, which you try to hide from others (shameless people do this by denial, by glorifying their shameful behavior in their own minds). Thoughts about the future evoke fantasies of glory, in which you revel in approbation and vindication from others and everybody is

What is Magic?

applauding you. Shame and glory are the carrot and stick which drive people in our society. We are all taught to hide our shame from other people, and to seek glory in their eyes. Hiding shame and seeking glory is the engine which motivates all our social striving. It is your thoughts of shame and glory which make you believe that you are separate and unique and special.

It's this constant internal dialogue of self-pity which makes you believe that there is a continuing, abiding "you" there. The constant thinking and agitation about a "you" is what creates that "you" – a shameful, glorious, shameful, glorious, shameful, glorious "you." That "you" doesn't even exist in the eyes of other people; it merely exists in your fantasies of how you imagine that other people see you. How much more flimsy could the thing be?

As you intend to stop pitying yourself – as you gradually lose your feelings of shame about the things which have happened to you, and your seeking glory in what might happen to you – you also lose your sense of there being a "you" there to whom things are happening. If you lose your sense of personal stake in what happens, then things no longer happen "to you"; they just happen, period (and you deal with them as best you can). Your lower self then begins to disintegrate. As it does so, your everyday, waking life becomes more like dreaming: more vivid and alive and full of meaning. That's when you step into the world of magic.

In contrast with your lower self, your higher self, or intent, has nothing whatever to do with your body (it transcends your personal death). Most people in their daily lives rarely operate with higher self. This is the purpose of magical training: to operate with higher self in your everyday existence.

In most people's lives higher self only surfaces now and then in response to emergencies and sudden, unexpected outside events (actually this is not true: it is in fact intent which creates the so-called "outside" events in the first place). Higher self surfaces to save your life; to pull you back from the brink; and to warn you away from certain people, situations, and places. Higher self sees an opportunity and grasps it without hesitation or doubt of any sort.

When you operate with your higher self, you are mentally clear, coldly efficient, pitilessly detached, and utterly determined. You no longer feel like your (usual, lower) self – trapped in your petty little moods and concerns. You are exhilarated and free; you become one with the Spirit.

When your higher self surfaces it brushes aside all your doubts and fears. You no longer fear death, and you never say die. Indeed, it is your higher self which survives the death of the physical body. This is why you don't fear death (or anything) when you act with your higher self.

In a manner of speaking, your higher self is actually the same thing as your death. When society teaches you fear of death, what it is teaching you is fear of your higher self. Your higher self is a state of unfettered limitlessness, just as your lower self is a state of crabbed dissatisfaction and torpor, symbolized by the prison of your body (with its endless cycle of needs and desires).

Your higher self acts from the gut, not the mind (this is literally true: our intent appears to consist of fibers of living light which are emitted from our navels). Indeed it can befuddle your thinking mind. The higher self doesn't operate on social conditioning – at least not in our decadent, self-indulgent society. Higher self was the basis of conditioning in warrior societies which existed on this earth in ancient times. Even as recently as a century ago humans were more robust, self-reliant, and daring (closer to higher self) than we self-coddling moderns are.

Your higher self acts on your true feelings, not on your thought forms. It acts on inner certainty rather than on the way you have been taught to act by your parents and society. As a result, when you act with your higher self, your own behavior may surprise or embarrass you. Your higher self can be quite audacious: sexual, defiant, or disruptive and contemptuous of social consequences. When your higher self takes command it takes your breath away. It numbs your lower self – your thinking mind – which feels somehow left out, embarrassed, guilty, or puzzled by your own actions.

What is Magic?

Your lower self may try to backpeddle, or make amends, or undo whatever social damage your higher self has perpetrated. It is at these moments that you can become conscious within yourself of the division between your lower and higher selves, since at such times they are both operating at once, at cross-purposes.

Both white and black magic involve an irreversible severing of ties to the world of people. Both paths entail stepping beyond the pale, beyond the fear-of-annihilation barrier which inhibits most people. In black magic the irrevocable commitment is made to doing evil – to rallying the lower self around a pitiless cruelty. In white magic the lower self is dissolved by relaxing into a pitiless indifference. Note that in both cases what the practitioner seeks to eliminate is pity: in black magic, pity for others; in white magic, self-pity.

It is the goal of magic, at least white magic, to step outside of the lower self and the body which symbolizes it. This necessitates overcoming your self-pity: not indulging your customary moods and concerns. White magicians try to cultivate the attitude that nothing that happens or doesn't happen is all that important.

This very sentiment is often expressed by people who lose part of their lower self willy-nilly after a near brush with death. They say things like, "Now, I'm just taking it one day at a time." What they are saying is that their eyeball-to-eyeball confrontation with their death has forced them to drop their customary moods and concerns. They lighten up, stop clinging to things, stop resenting the past and worrying about the future. They become more selfless.

Selflessness means that, while both good and bad things still happen to the person, there's not as much of a "me" there that things are happening to. There's less personal stake in what happens. Situations just unfold under their own momentum. Things are taken in stride – philosophically, not personally. There is no way to fake this attitude (e.g., by "thinking happy thoughts", which is actually a form of denial). It has to come of its own after years and years of painstaking inner work and the daily resort to nature spirits (although as noted above a near-death experience can induce this attitude as well).

Erasing the lower self is not easy or fun; indeed, it's quite painful. St. John of the Cross characterized it as the Dark Night of the Soul. Since it is your mind, your constant thinking, which stabilizes your reality and which brings the world into focus, in order to become a magician you literally have to lose your mind. Most magicians go through a period in which they fear that they are going crazy. Carlos Castaneda, for example, described this period in his training by don Juan.

I had something similar happen to me. I'm a mathematician and computer programmer and for almost a year I couldn't muster the concentration necessary to program. I was worried that I was losing my mind permanently. To prove to myself that I could still think, I forced myself to work out a detailed algorithm which took me many months longer than it would have normally. This difficulty in focusing my attention passed, but I still have periods in which I can scarcely concentrate. I know now that at these times I shouldn't try to program unless I absolutely have to. I realize now that these kinds of mental lapses are normal. Becoming a magician means letting go of everything that you cling to; and of course sanity is one of those things.

Another way of looking at the lower self is to think of it as consisting of concentric rings of decreasing importance, like the layers of an onion. The brain is at the center. The rest of the body forms the next ring. Possessions and intimate relationships form another ring. Religion, country, hobbies, favorite sports team are an outer ring; and so on. If any of these rings are threatened, then most people feel that their lower self is threatened. Take, as an example, how most Americans felt about the attack on the World Trade Center in 2001. They felt as though they, personally, had been attacked. Thus it is true to say that to most Americans, the World Trade Center was a part of what they considered to be their self.

To a magician, however, the self is everything. In other words, to get to your higher self, instead of using your brain and body as a central point of reference, you use the world as a

What is Magic?

whole. To actually make this shift is not an intellectual feat but an emotional one. It involves opening your heart – having compassion for everything instead of just your onion rings. To connect to your higher self, try using this Creative Visualization:

> Feel that you are truly connected to the universe;
> That you have been chosen to save the world;
> That you have been chosen to reach out to and bless every being that comes in contact with you;
> That your love knows no bounds and gives you joy such as you never thought was possible.

Then go on to visualize how this is being expressed in ways that you would prefer. You can alter the basic formula at will to make it more meaningful to you personally. Do this visualization twice daily. You should become imbued with this visualization, thinking and feeling it all day long, like daydreaming, but in the present tense.

Also every day you must sense your connectedness to all that is around you and to everyone you meet. Reject nothing and no one who comes your way. Little-by-little you'll take possession of your higher self and shed the lower one.

IX – Bewitching

Magic is a craft. It's something you learn. Magicians usually do have supernormal powers, but these powers are learned. There can be inborn talent, but it takes a lifetime of practice just to perfect one such power. This is why the terms "occultism", "secret science", "mysticism", and so forth are silly. There is nothing secret or hidden going on here. Magic is merely a matter of paying conscious attention to the things which society has taught you to ignore, fear, or disbelieve.

Magic is what everyone is doing all the time, beneath the surface of everyday life. Most people just pretend they aren't doing it; or else they don't consider what they do to be magic, or they don't even realize they are doing it. For example, infatuation is a species of mutual bewitching. Lovers bewitch one another and themselves. But they wouldn't consider this magic. They consider it "love" – at least until the bewitchment, the infatuation, wears off.

Similarly, people who cannot break free of an abusive relationship are usually bewitched by their partners. Doctors, and all healers, cure people by stimulating and encouraging the people's own faith in getting well. Good salespeople are adept at bewitching their customers. And so on.

Everyone is manipulating everyone else on a magical level all the time. Any time people command another's attention, or manipulate their feelings in any way, they are bewitching them. Thus all art is magic, and great artists are merely great magicians. Artists are highly intuitive people who can tune into profound feelings in their art and take other people with them.

Magicians are perhaps a bit more psychic to start with than average people. At least magicians rely upon and trust in their intuition more than average people do. To most people, psychic events such as precognition, prophetic dreams, omens, telepathic communications happen now and then unbidden, but are beyond conscious control. Such things happen to magicians with somewhat more frequency because magicians welcome, or intend, such things – or better said, magicians pay

What is Magic?

more attention to the little nuances in everyday life which most people miss in their mindless scurrying about. With some experience and practice magicians learn to control their psychic abilities.

For example, when faced with a problem, one thing many magicians do is to pray (intend) upon retiring at night for the solution to their problem to come to them. With a little practice they find that this works most of the time. They receive the answer in a dream that night, or else it comes in the next day or two, through some chance happening or offhand remark by someone. And as they see this technique work time and time again, it builds their faith; and as their faith builds the technique keeps working better and better for them.

Faith, the emotional content of belief, is the key to making magic work. It can move mountains. It is the lever by which you create your own reality. The only reason your thought form world works is because you put your faith in it. If you believed in magic with the same certainty that you believe turning a key in an ignition will start a car, then magic would work as well for you as science and technology do.

That's what faith is all about. There have been societies on this earth which were based upon magic, such as the Mayan Indians of Central America. These societies get magic to work for them as well as materialistic science does for us, because that's where they put their faith.

The reasons why magic often doesn't work as well as the books, and one's own spirit guides, for that matter, say that it should, are sundry. Sometimes it just isn't time yet. "To everything there is a season." All the prayers and spells in the world won't make Christmas happen before December 25th. Sometimes your prayers and spells are contingent upon the right astrological influence occurring.

Other times your prayers and spells don't work right away because you have heavy karma in the way that has to be cleaned out first. This karmic barrier to realizing your desires might stem from previous lifetimes, as well as this one. In my own case it took twenty years of just putting in the time and paying my dues between when I first made the decision to follow the magician's path and when my spirit guides appeared in my life, which was my actual entry into the world of magic. From there it was another twenty-five years until I started seeing some real results from magic working on my own, without spirits backing me up. However, I never lost faith, and that's why I have succeeded so far.

The difference between magicians and average people is that magicians have infinite patience and a willingness to confront any danger and endure any pain necessary in order to realize their desires. Average people, on the other hand, always seem to be looking for a free ride or handout in life. Average people's decisions don't have enough power behind them to accomplish anything worthwhile because they back down and reverse their decisions the minute the going gets a little tough. What helped me a lot in my own quest, I see now in retrospect, was that my situation was truly desperate and miserable. I had nothing to go back to, so I had no choice but to press forward.

The Spirit always plays little games on your head to test you in your resolve. It always makes it as difficult as possible to stand by your decisions. Things never happen the way you fantasize them or rehearse them in your daydreams. Average people are ready to throw in the towel and weep in self-pity at every little disappointment. Magicians know that once a decision has been made, there's no going back unless the Spirit itself grants release. The basic principles of magic – of intent – are to make absolutely irrevocable decisions; and then to go to any extreme necessary to stand by those decisions.

Power is the same thing as luck. True luck involves leaving nothing to chance. Average people, if they believe in magic at all, believe that magicians control chance. This isn't correct. Magicians, at least white magicians, don't dominate chance or enforce their own will on the universe. Rather, they are wholly dominated by it. They give up all personal expectations of their own, cease caring whether they win or lose, or get their own way or not (they don't give up wanting things; they just give up their sense of stake in whether the things happen or not). In this way magicians become one with chance and merge themselves with it. Then their will becomes unstoppable.

What is Magic?

Magicians will to accept the Spirit's will as their own. They give up all their own images of what they think they desire and let the Spirit's desires for them prevail. When magicians synchronize their own desires with those of the Spirit, everything becomes possible for them. The great enemy of magic is doubt.

I happen to have the power to bewitch women to fall in love with me (okay, no snickering out there, this happens to be true). My spirits taught me how to do this to show me that magic does indeed work – that it is possible to make impossible things happen merely by willing it. They also wanted to teach me to hold my attention fixed upon a single object, moment-to-moment, all day long every day. They know me pretty well: they knew that the only thing that would motivate me to put out the effort and discipline needed to do this was the promise of sex.

I'll save the details of my experiences with bewitching women for my autobiography, except to say that the last time I tried it, it backfired on me in such a way that I'll never do it again. Besides, although you can get sex by bewitching, you can't get love that way, so why bother?

Psychic healing works the same way that bewitching does. The healer visualizes the patient as being well, and thus overrides the patient's doubt and self-pity. It's also possible to bewitch to stun: to disarm an angry or threatening person (or just to shut someone up) by disorienting and befuddling them (I don't know how to do this, but I've had it done to me). Any form of ensorcellment involves substituting the magician's will for the subject's will. This can only take place if the subject is willing, consciously or unconsciously. That is to say, no one can be bewitched, or healed, against their will.

Bewitching is really no different than Creative Visualization. Magicians know to keep their Creative Visualizations within the realm of reasonable possibility. Thus they don't try to bewitch famous movie stars to fall in love with them, or to win the lottery. These sorts of outcomes are too unlikely. In order to make magic work it is necessary to overcome doubt, and wishing for something that's way out of your league, or too improbable, starts off with too big a doubt debit.

When bewitching for love, for example, magicians start out with someone with whom they already have desire lines in place. This means someone with whom they have already shared feelings; someone they've already looked directly in the eye and flashed with. That flash doesn't necessarily have to have been one of love. The flash could have been anger, disgust, humor, or sadness as well as attraction. It doesn't matter. If, for an instant, two people look in each other's eyes and some emotion passes between them, then at that moment they stuck lines in each another. They bewitched one another. If there is any feeling at all between two people, whether positive or negative, then they can be bewitched through that feeling.

What passes in brief moments of direct eye contact is very powerful sexual magic. It is so potent, in fact, that it scares most people. They immediately get flustered, avert their eyes, and pretend that nothing happened. Even when the emotion that is being shared is humor or gaiety, there is a polite limit to how long direct eye contact can be engaged before it becomes threatening, i.e. sexual. Even if the emotion is anger or disgust, that just means that the feeling is so sexual that it has to be hidden by its negation.

Sexual feeling is the matrix of all feeling. Sexual feelings are actual lines which people shoot into one another, like arrows, whenever they flash on each other by sharing a feeling. These lines appear to people with psychic vision as fibers of living light. It's through the light fibers which join people that they pass emotional information, such as the psychic knowledge that the other person is hurt, or dead, or having sex with someone else. It's also through these light fibers that bewitching takes place (see the drawings of humans interacting on a light fiber level in Barbara Brennan's book *Light Emerging*[1]).

In short, if two people have ever shared any direct feeling, then there's already a sexual bond between them. Magicians can use this bond to bewitch, or to heal. They force energy through that desire line by intense visualization of their

What is Magic?

desire coming true. This brings pressure to bear upon the interpersonal barrier. This barrier is the pretense that there's nothing going on between the participants.

Sexual desire can exist from previous lifetimes and realities – this is usually what's behind the phenomenon of love at first sight. If there's an underlying sexual attraction (which can in fact be read from the natal horoscopes of the people involved) then there's fertile ground for bewitching even if the two people have not yet met face-to-face.

On the surface, the magicians act cordially but disinterestedly. They keep a poker face and they do nothing on their own account. Eventually that pressure brings about a moment in time when the Spirit itself opens the floodgates and the other person's defenses evaporate. If and when it's time for an overt move, it comes on its own in a moment of power.

In everyday society most of the actual sticking of desire lines into other people is done in the state of dreamless sleep, although the intent is set up in waking. If you have ever had a dream war with someone, that person was trying to stick a line into you, but you successfully fought them off. If you hadn't successfully fought them off, you wouldn't have had that dream. It would have remained unconscious, on the level of dreamless sleep.

Magicians, both black and white, sometimes rely upon spirit helpers to cue them on what to do and when. These messages come across as sudden ideas or inspirations. But magicians don't act unless prompted.

In other words the magicians' superficial behavior betrays nothing of what they are actually thinking or feeling. Contrast this with how average people try to make their desires come true. Average people get caught up in making obvious moves, polishing their self-presentation, trying to somehow flag other people's, or God's, attention: "Yoo-hoo! Here I am! Over here!"

This approach will work sometimes, but it's really inept. This is what the dating game is all about, which is why people find it so boring and predictable. There's no sport to it. Besides there's no true feeling to it, much less love. It's all phony.

When magicians bewitch, all their energy is held rigidly in check. Desire is inflamed by visualization, which is why magic is basically a matter of bewitching yourself. Magic is hypnotizing yourself into an intense, single-pointed desire. Magicians first have to bewitch themselves to be madly in love – they go first. Then they impose that feeling on the subject of their desire. Better said, they give the subject a powerful option.

No one can be forced to do anything against his or her own will by magic. It's quite possible for the person being bewitched to block the ensorcellment by detaching his or her light fibers from the magician. This is felt as closing up to them emotionally. What magicians, particularly black magicians, count on is that most people's wills are so weak and confused.

Magicians may use some object symbolic of their desire and pour all of their attention on it. They imagine the face of the person in it and talk with it and make love with it and cuddle with it at night. For example, in the movie *Bell, Book and Candle*, Kim Novak bewitched Jimmy Stewart with a cat. In the book *The Witch's Dream* by Florinda Donner, the protagonist bewitched his love with a devil's mask. The symbolic object can be charged like a charm.

Thus bewitching is like normal daydreaming or fantasizing, carried to an extreme. When bewitching for love, the magician visualizes him or herself in the presence of the beloved – holding hands, kissing and caressing, having fun together – as if the person were actually there. In bewitching you look the other person (the lover you desire, the boss you want a raise from, the enemy you want to get rid of) directly in the eye. In normal daydreaming and fantasizing, by contrast, you're usually not making eye contact at all. In bewitching the focus is on the other person and how enjoyable it is to be in their company (or to be rid of them, depending upon what you are bewitching for). In normal daydreaming the focus is on yourself, and other people serve only as mute witnesses to your own glory and vindication. This is the difference between bewitching and fanning the breeze with idle daydreaming. When you bewitch someone you're right there

What is Magic?

in front of them eyeball-to-eyeball. You let them do the talking and make the moves. In daydreaming they're fawning over you while you carry on a monologue.

This is another difference between Creative Visualization, what magicians do, and fantasizing and daydreaming, which average people do. Visualization is a matter of feeling, of longing, of reaching out for the object of desire. Daydreaming is a matter of conceptualizing, imaging, distancing yourself from the object of desire, pushing it away to a future which never comes. Daydreaming is actually reaching out towards self-pity, not towards the realization of your true desires.

You should not daydream or have romantic or sexual fantasies about someone whom you are bewitching. They will feel this through the light fibers you have in them as a sleazy vibe, a sexual expectation, coming from you; and they will raise defenses against it. Creative Visualization, true bewitching, usually doesn't have a context of sexual or romantic excitation at all. It's too here-and-now, too spontaneous and unpredictable. It has a light, joyous feeling to it as compared to the obsessive and directed intensity of most daydreaming. Daydreams are about control, whereas Creative Visualization is about joy.

When bewitching to get rid of someone, magicians don't visualize bad things happening to that person. Rather, they visualize themselves happy, relieved, joyous, now that this person is gone. Psychic healing is done by visualizing the person as well. The point is that the visualization has to be done as if the action is unfolding in the here and now, unlike normal daydreams, which take place in the future. One has to feel all the feelings – joy, relief, health, whatever – that would be felt if the visualization were actually true. It's those feelings which are being felt which attract the object of desire; which make the visualization come true.

Conscious awareness is where all links ultimately have to be made. A magician, however, never makes links through direct intervention, by acting on his or her own accord. This is how average people blow things or trip themselves up. They fail by acting on their thought forms, by being impatient and pushy, by being unwilling or unable to trust in the Spirit to bring them what they want in the fullness of time. This shows lack of faith. Only the Spirit can move the wheel of chance. Therefore the basic principle of magic is patience.

Everybody already knows intuitively how to make magic work, but they don't do it much since if they succeeded they'd scare themselves silly. This is another difference between daydreaming and Creative Visualization. In daydreaming the person doesn't really want the desire to come true. He or she is just playing games, fanning the breeze. Therefore it usually takes an intense, overwhelming desire or desperation to activate average people's true magical powers. Miracles do sometimes happen, when people are 100% clear in their intent – when they permit their higher self to surface and take command. Magicians strive to make every moment a miracle.

Creative Visualization is the same thing as prayer. Everyone intuitively understands the efficacy of prayer, but most people don't call upon it unless they're desperate. However, desperation isn't the best motivation for prayer since people create their own realities. They wouldn't be in that situation in the first place unless they created it for some reason, to learn some lesson. If that lesson happens to be learning the power of faith, that prayer does work, then their prayers will save their butts; but not necessarily otherwise.

The problem with magic as a spiritual path, and bewitching people in particular, is that it hangs us up in all the same stupid games of winning and losing that are played out in everyday society (this is what I ultimately learned from my experiences with ensorcellment – that it's childish). The only difference is that magicians aim to be winners, whereas average people aim to be losers – to wallow in helplessness and self-pity.

Fundamentally magic is as much a dead-end street for an aspirant on the spiritual path as is seeking the validation and glory of society. The only value to magic, which seems baffling at first but which is learned through experience, by making lots of mistakes, is understanding the difference between when one is acting on one's own impulse, or when one is truly being prompted to act by the Spirit. This is the crux of the matter, and the reason why learning magic is worthwhile.

Notes:

[1] Brennan, Barbara, *Light Emerging*, Bantam NYC 1993

X – Magic and Money

The magicians' view of money is that human beings have been on this earth for around two million years; our species, *Homo sapiens*, has been around for 200,000 years; but money has only existed for 3,000 years. Somehow or other humans got along quite well without money for most of their existence. Therefore money must not be an indispensable prerequisite for human life to carry on.

This is the magicians' view of money, as contrasted with average people's view, that money is right up there in importance with air and water. This addresses the question, if magicians are so powerful, why ain't they rich? The answer is that magic, at least white magic, isn't about making all your desires come true. It's about reducing your desires to a bare minimum. To a magician, enough is enough. It's plenty, in fact.

Most people's sense of self-esteem and self-worth, feeling good about themselves, are tied up with how other people see them. This means how much money they have, or how much approval and approbation they are getting from others, especially from people of the opposite sex.

People's worry about not having enough money is actually worry about not measuring up. Their fear of not having enough money is actually fear of permitting themselves to be happy, because underneath they believe that they are not deserving of happiness. In other words, it's not really about money at all. Money is just the presenting problem which obscures an underlying psychological issue of low self-esteem.

Magicians allow themselves to be happy *now*, no matter how much money they have or don't have. They find a way to be happy in the now moment, by taking joy in the sounds of bird calls or the feel of the breeze on their faces. Like most people, their sense of self-worth depends upon how much they have; but magicians believe that they've already got it all. At least, they've got everything they need.

To become a magician, then, doesn't mean waving a magic wand and chanting a spell and all this money comes to

What is Magic? 113

you. Rather it means weaning yourself away from worrying about money by simply refusing to worry about it. This is an act of intent. It means putting the bills on your desk aside and looking out the window at the children playing next door, and taking joy in that one. When you can feel happy now, money tends to take care of itself. Poverty isn't particularly pleasant, but it does teach you to appreciate little things. Rich people never know that feeling.

One trick magicians use (and magic is nothing if not tricking yourself, as its critics rightly point out) is rather than comparing yourself to people who are better off than you are, to feed your jealousy and self-pity, instead to compare yourself to people (like 95% of the world's population) who are worse off than you are, to feed your gratitude and appreciation.

Another trick magicians use to overcome money problems is to think about their deaths. Magicians are acutely aware of the fact that when they die, they won't be taking their money or money worries with them. They will, however, be taking their joy and satisfaction in a life well-lived with them. Being a magician means being very selective about what baggage you decide to carry along with you in life. Money and possessions and their attendant worries are burdens which most magicians find too heavy to schlep.

I recently read a book by the Peruvian economist Hernando de Soto entitled *The Mystery of Capital*. This is an excellent exposition of what capital is and how it is formed, with particular reference to problems faced by the urban poor in developing nations. It occurred to me that de Soto's conclusions wouldn't apply to the rural poor – at least not to my Mayan Indian neighbors. This is because they aren't interested in money per se. It's not that they like being poor, but rather to them freedom is more important than money. To the Maya, family, religion, and maize constitute wealth. Money is something that you scrabble around for as it is needed. It's not something to amass for its own sake or for a rainy day. They use faith and reliance on God for their rainy days. If God doesn't come through for them, that's life in the tropics.

Poor people, on average, tend to be happier than rich people. At least this is true in agrarian cultures – not in First World society, where the urban poor have their poverty rubbed in their faces every day. This is because poor people have fewer expectations than rich people. It doesn't take as much for them to be happy. They find happiness in owning less rather than more, because less is what they've got. They've learned the trick of finding happiness in the now moment, because the now moment is all they own. Having fewer expectations implies greater happiness with what you have, rather than dwelling upon what you lack.

It's hard for twenty-first century First Worlders to understand how it is that they don't own possessions, but rather possessions own them. As the poet said, when you got nothin' you got nothin' to lose. This is quite true, as the Maya understand.

Possessions are actually alive, and like all living things they try to multiply.[1] Possessions voraciously demand more and more possessions. You become the slave of your possessions: the more possessions you own, the more possessions you desire. You become a mere instrument in the multiplication of your possessions; a mindless robot under the control and direction of your possessions.

Nobody needs all the crap which most people have in their living rooms and kitchens, not to mention piled up in their attics, basements, and garages. Shopping and shameless pigging out on possessions are a rather sorry substitute for true joy and fulfillment; but that's about all many people in our society know. It's a shame that we have to spend our entire adult lives undoing the conditioning that was foisted upon us in our early childhoods. Imagine what our society could be like if people were raised to be happy and accepting of themselves rather than robotic producer / consumers trapped in a spiral of insatiable desire and dissatisfaction. All of our energy could be spent on creative and spiritually uplifting concerns rather than in paying tribute to our demon masters.

To be a capitalist means tying yourself to an artificial system. Your sense of well-being and self-esteem go up and down with that system. While the system is working, you're

What is Magic?

in fat city. When the system fails you get laid off; or your securities plummet; or you're forced into bankruptcy.

This system is going to fail. There is an economic term for the fabulous amassing of wealth which has occurred in the First World over the past half-century: it's called a bubble (n.b., this was written before the recent economic crisis). We can see the collapse happening already in irreversible climatic changes. Capitalism is a pyramid scheme. The capitalist system as it is presently constituted is predicated upon the myth that it can continue to rip off the earth and its people forever. This isn't so, it's just been lucky so far. Humanity is not going to be able to muddle through this one as it has always done before.

The magician's quarrel with capitalism isn't the inherent unfairness and injustice built into it. That's just the way life is, the way nature is (which is the tune the capitalists sing to justify their shameless avarice; and they are quite correct – the universe is a predatorial place). There's nothing anyone can do about that. Rather, the magician's criticism of capitalism is that it's about to self-destruct and drag the human race and the earth herself down with it.

Capitalism is turning this earth into a hell world. Insatiable greed, the basis of capitalism, is not an innate human character trait. There have been human societies in which greed and self-indulgence were not the principle mainsprings to all action. Indeed, in spiritual societies to this day, such as the Mayan Indians, unbridled selfishness is discouraged or viewed as aberrant behavior; and the society has built-in mechanisms to keep everyone on more or less the same economic level.[2] The usual pro-capitalist argument runs that capitalism has succeeded in delivering the goods to much of the human population on earth. And what is suggested as an alternative? The answer to that one is that capitalism is working now (poorly), but it won't be able to keep it up, or else the price in human misery and the destruction of the earth will become prohibitive.

The capitalist system will change when enough people, as individuals, stop voting for it. Just as people have learned to use possessions to prop up their lack of true self-esteem, they can unlearn this. What I suggest as an alternative to capitalism is magic: people listening to their hearts. From the magical point of view possessions are actually a bring-down, a trap. People can understand this by listening to their own hearts, not to what the media and advertisers and their peers are trying to convince them that they need and want

Some people say that it is naïve to expect human nature to change. But the basis of capitalism as it is today – unbridled selfishness and short-sighted stupidity – is not human nature. It's demon nature. There was a time before humans allied themselves with demons, and not so long ago, either (12,000 years ago when agriculture was invented). Hunting / gathering societies to this day are not usually based upon selfishness and greed, but upon a sense of group well-being. We modern humans have just become so imbued with the assumptions of demonism that we cannot conceive of a social order based on anything other than distrust and rapacity.

This is because of lack of faith. Our society has taught us that magic doesn't exist. Even though most people in their heart of hearts know that this is untrue, still it takes a lot of inner work to overcome that doubt about magic. If most people in our society were as focused on magic as they are on making money, magic would work very well, as it once did in many ancient societies and still does for the Maya. However, some ancient societies based on magic turned to black magic – not that our present money-grubbing society doesn't perform human sacrifice in order to protect oiling drilling rights, etc. This is what tends to happen when demons are allowed to run things.

Most people are the slaves of uncontrolled desire. Gazing into store windows, strolling through the supermarket, watching advertisements on television or the internet, they shoot out so many desire lines at so many things they don't really want, that it's little wonder that they can't bring any of them into manifestation. And if they can, they lose interest in the objects of their desire the minute they possess them; then they desire some new object. It's not the putative objects of their desire which people desire, but rather the state of desire itself. It's the constant hunger, the feeling of incompleteness, that drives most people forward (this is what W.B. Yeats termed "Deception", and we term "striving"). By contrast magicians, both white and black, concentrate all their desires on one single object which symbolizes power. Magicians don't waste energy coveting trinkets which are not going to augment their power.

The fewer expectations you have, the happier you are. The more expectations you have, the unhappier you are. It doesn't matter whether your expectations are fulfilled or not, whether you are rich or poor, since a fulfilled expectation is quickly replaced by a new expectation. The key to happiness, then, is to reduce your expectations rather than to devise ways and means of fulfilling your expectations.

I have some young magician friends who have doubts about magic (even though in their hearts they realize its truth) because they've never gotten it to work on a material plane. I don't blame them. Until you see actual results, faith is rather hollow. Faith is not blind. We magicians have no use for blind faith. We are the ultimate result merchants, from Missouri, "Show me!" We believe when we see results. Our faith is based on the positive results of past experience.

Faith is not the same thing as belief. Belief is an intellectual construct, whereas faith is a matter of the heart. Faith can be based on belief – indeed it has to be – but it is basically a matter of intent. You create your own reality. It is what you have faith in that creates your reality.

If you have faith in the capitalist system, then that is your reality. That's what you've bought into. A magician doesn't buy into any intellectual construct, because to a magician all intellection is *prima facie* false. Magicians are operating, or trying to operate, on a different guidance system altogether. They listen to their own hearts. They operate on intent, intuition, direct knowing and understanding, rather than on what anyone else thinks or has taught them to think. To magicians, thinking is beside the point. It's what they feel in their hearts that matters.

This is hard to do in twenty-first century First World society, because everything points the opposite way. The high priests of our society – the politicians, media manipulators, bankers, academics, and so forth – put their faith in something altogether different. They try to teach you to do the same. There are no social rewards for following the impulses of your own heart. Job interviewers don't say "Wow – great! You are just what we're looking for – someone who follows their own heart! We don't want mindless robots who will follow orders blindly and do what they're told without question. We want robust individuals who will follow their own hearts!"

Having faith – true faith – means flying in the face of everything which you've been taught all your life. It means following your heart in spite of the opposition and rejection of your family, friends, and society. It means seeking your sense of security in what your heart knows is true – not in pieces of paper and empty promises. If you can do that, you'll succeed on the magician's path. In fact, it's guaranteed.

Magicians who want to get money to come to them analyze objectively, not enviously, people who are successful at getting money to come to them. They isolate the mechanism involved. What distinguishes financially successful people like Bill Gates and Ted Turner?

The answer is that such people, even when they're down and out, know that the money will come. They take their present lack of money in their stride. Whether this faith is innate or learned from experience, they know in their hearts that the money will come.

Their attitude is an object lesson for all of us in what our attitude towards money should be. It's not like, "When the money comes then I'll stop worrying about it." which is what we tell ourselves. No, the truth is that the mechanism works the other way around. When you stop worrying about it, then the money comes.

Worrying about money, fantasizing about money, buying lottery tickets are, like magical techniques such as Creative Visualization, commands to the universe. However, they are commands of lack rather than fulfillment. They don't have the confidence, the true faith, behind them of true commands to the Spirit. What these piddling commands are actually calling up is self-pity – excuses to pity yourself (moaning and groaning, or feeling jealous of wealthier people).

What is Magic?

How do you stop worrying about money? There is indeed a Law of Abundance, but this Law has a catch to it that they don't tell you about – namely that there is also a Law of Karma. Until the Law of Karma is covered, the Law of Abundance is overridden. The main reason why people's spells and prayers don't work is because on some level or other they don't want them to work. Perhaps they feel unworthy; or for whatever reason they have issues which they must work out before they can allow themselves to feel free. This is where inner work is invaluable.[3] You have to analyze yourself and your history and figure out why you got yourself into this money worry trap in the first place. You weren't born with it. What does money symbolize to you? Why is your self-esteem so low or your self-pity so high that you have to fret over money, instead of feeling good about yourself and your circumstances right this minute? Why are you not grateful for all that you have already, reveling in the sunlight and the whisper of the wind blowing through the trees? That's all you needed when you were little. At some point in your life you decided to torture yourself over money. This stand was not imposed upon you against your will, no matter what you believe and are telling yourself now. This is the purpose of inner work – to find that information out.

Until you find out exactly how you are tripping yourself up, keeping yourself in an uptight money situation to prove some stupid point to yourself, you will not be able to get out of it, no matter how many Creative Visualizations of Abundance you do. Why are you putting yourself in that situation? What is your pay-off? What hole in your self-esteem are you trying to plug with money and possessions? When you understand the answers to these questions, then you can stop worrying about money. And then the money will come.

Notes:

[1] In the Mayan worldview not all possessions possess souls (consciousness). Only foodstuffs (especially maize), tools related to food production (hoe, machete, grindstone, pots, fire), certain functional items such as hammock and

broom; and religious / ceremonial items (such as crosses and musical instruments) are considered to be alive and to require special, respectful treatment or propitiation. In the magical worldview, anything we obsess over becomes alive and takes possession of us; and most First Worlders obsess over possessions.

[2] Mayan society has built-in mechanisms to keep everyone on the same economic level – such as the social incumbency upon people who attain a superior degree of wealth to throw a religious celebration for the entire community, which returns the host family to poverty. Obviously such a society can't "progress" much economically; all it can do is preserve its dignity, its soul, and its sense of higher purpose, which our capitalistic society has completely lost.

[3] Inner work can be done through therapy; or more cheaply on your own using a technique such as Carl Jung's Active Imagination. See my book *Thought Forms*, or Robert A. Johnson's book *Inner Work* (Harper & Row, San Francisco, 1986) for more information.

XI – Death

The magicians' view of things is usually the exact opposite of average people's view. What average people call reality, magicians call illusion. What average people consider desirable, magicians consider worthless. What average people call truth, magicians call lies. Similarly, death from the point of view of magic is very different from death as it is commonly understood.

When you listen to sounds, you can distinguish between two phenomena: "sounds" and "listener listening to sounds".

"Sounds" is when you are hearing all sounds indiscriminately, like a tape recorder does; when all sounds are impacting on your awareness with equal vividness. This is how infants hear things; and how we adults can hear them when we are very relaxed.

"Listener listening to sounds" is when you are focusing on one specific sound, and the other sounds are in the background of your awareness.

That "listener listening to sounds"– that focus, or the sense of there being a detached perceiver who is perceiving – is what magicians call lower self. At least, that is what dies when your body dies. When there is no longer a sense of a separated perceiver perceiving, when everything is impacting upon your awareness with equal vividness, what is left is a feeling of oneness, a background of peacefulness, which is what magicians call higher self, or death. Death is in the background all the time. Death is the canvas upon which your life is painted.

In dreams there is no death. You can never die in dreams – you just wake up. There is no death because perception takes place directly, without so much sense of an intermediary or detached perceiver who is perceiving. Everything is so vivid and intense that you are more caught up in events than you are when you are awake (and detached from what is going on around you).

In dreams you do still have a limited sense of lower self. This is symbolized by a body: a center or sense of a "you" to whom things are happening. In other words, lower self can still exist in an environment such as dreaming in which death does not exist. However, there isn't as much lower self in dreaming as there is when you're awake. You're not as "you" in dreams.

You don't have as much lower self when you dream because you don't do much thinking in dreaming, just as you don't die. Your ability to think, and your body – together with your body's death – arise together. They're two aspects of the same phenomenon.

It can be argued that infants and primitive people die even though they don't think much. This isn't really true. Death doesn't have the same meaning for infants or primitive people that it has for us. Infants and primitive people live with their past lives and their ancestors in a sense that we modern adults can scarcely comprehend. They are less separated, more rooted in something which is greater than the individual. They are less individuated than modern adults, and as a result feel less anguish of separatedness (they feel more joy of connectedness) in their everyday lives as compared with modern adults.

Infants and primitive people don't feel as much difference as modern adults do between being awake and dreaming; or between being alive and being dead. Primitives palpably feel the presence of their ancestors and dead loved ones, and they communicate back-and-forth with them for guidance and blessing. Their world is less solid; more like dreaming; more ineffable and magical than ours is. Infants and primitive people don't think as much, or as well, as we do. They can't problem-solve as well as we can because they lack our ability to focus that much attention. But they don't live or die as we do, either. They have more sense of being part of an ongoing process. They don't feel as isolated and anguished in both their lives and their deaths as we do.

Similarly, animals don't die as adult humans do. The idea that animals die in a similar way to humans is pure anthropomorphism. We humans don't have a clue as to how other species perceive the world. Other species' perceptions and cognition are so alien to the human way of perceiving and

What is Magic?

making sense of things that we adult humans can't conceive of it. Yes, we are all here together in this so-called reality; but animals pick up such different information from the environment than we humans do, and interpret it in such a different way, that for the most part it may as well be considered an entirely different universe. Animal perception and cognition are vaguely like how you perceive the world when you're dreaming, but even more so. Much more so.

The physical body is a just a symbol for the sense of perceiver perceiving. The physical body doesn't exist in any objective sense, any more than the body that you have in dreams exists except in the context of a given dream. The particular form that this sense of perceiver perceiving takes depends upon the particular human culture and *Zeitgeist*.

If you could time-travel to a previous century you would be thoroughly disoriented (and the further back you went, the more disoriented you would feel), since you wouldn't be able to grasp the thought form structure of the times. It would be like going to a foreign country and culture, but more so. You don't realize how much you depend on all the other humans around you to make sense out of the world: to make sense out of what you are perceiving.

It takes years and years for babies to learn how to do this. Babies little-by-little plug into human society, which on the one hand enables them to make some kind of sense out of what they are experiencing, but which also plugs them into their death.

In other words, from the magicians' point of view, there's a lot more to death than just vacating your body and becoming stiff. This is because the body isn't what it appears to be. How many people witnessed the 1917 epiphany of the Virgin of Fatima? How many people, looking at that same vision, saw nothing?

Our perception and cognition, over hundreds of millennia of human evolution as predators, have been biased in the direction of our senses, particular the visual sense. Quite naturally, therefore, any information coming into the system will be interpreted as sensory even if the senses have nothing to do with it.

Don't you still have sensory input in dreams? Is anyone going to argue that dreams are therefore real? Then on what basis can it be argued that the everyday world is real? Your only criterion for its reality is based on sensory input. And on what basis can your body be considered real?

In the same way that you consider your body solid and real, you are already biased towards a certain interpretation of what death is. You are under the impression that "you" will die, when in fact all that dies is your sense of self as separated perceiver. But your perception doesn't die. Only your body dies, but your body is no more intimately connected to your true, higher self than the clothes you wear.

One of a magician's first tasks is to eradicate fear of death. Fear of death is necessary for average people, to keep them out of trouble, such as crossing the street when the light is red. People are taught to fear death by their parents and society. To deny that fear, they're taught that they'll go to heaven when they die. Magicians, on the other hand, use moment-to-moment awareness of what's happening to keep them out of trouble. To magicians, fear of death, and the lies piled on top of that fear to cover it up, become excess baggage.

The way to overcome fear of death is to look squarely at it. It's part of life, there's no way around it. You chose it when you chose to be born. What's the big deal?

Moreover, the moment of death is completely overwhelming. At the moment of death things happen so fast, you're so swept up and carried away, that there's no space to emotionally react. Like in the few seconds before an accident, there's not enough separation between perceiver and what is being perceived for fear to exist. There's not enough "you" (lower self) there when you die, to feel fear. So when you fear death you are not actually fearing what you will feel when you die. Rather, you are fearing your fear.

People do not fear death qua death. Rather, what they fear is their fear of death. Feeling fear is a perfectly normal reaction, and there's nothing wrong with it. However, feeling fear of fear is neurosis. Fear of death, unless death is

What is Magic?

imminent, is feeling fear of fear. It's the entrance into an endless loop – the loop of enslavement by society.

Overcoming fear of death, then, is a matter of overcoming fear of fear. This is accomplished by looking squarely and rationally at all the nonfearful things which your society has trained you to fear. In particular you must eradicate your fear of what other people might think of you. A good place to start doing this is to take a good, straight look at your own true sexual desires (see the later chapter on "Magic and Sex").

The problem with the belief in going to heaven when you die, besides sidetracking you from overcoming your fear of death by facing it directly, is that it tends to inflate self-importance and complacency. This is precisely what magicians are trying to eradicate. Moreover, there is nothing in the Christian Bible, even granting that the Bible is correct on this point (which magicians don't concede), that says that heaven is a place where people go when they die. There are various references to a final resurrection at the end of time, but all references to heaven in the Bible can be and should be interpreted as a state of mind, not as a place where the soul goes after death.[1]

There's no point in arguing about this, but consider the following: it is sometimes said that Jews are smarter than other people. The fact is that they aren't, of course. However Jews do have an intellectual edge over most Christians and Muslims, and that edge is that *they are not hampered by a belief system*. Jews aren't smarter than anyone else; they're just not indoctrinated from infancy to shut down their thinking processes and unquestioningly accept pat, simplistic answers to life's deepest questions. As Leo Rosten put it: "It may be said that Jews lost their faith so easily because they had no faith to lose: that is, they had no doctrine, no collection of dogmas to which they could cling and with which they could resist argument. All they had, surrounding them like an armor, was a complete set of practices, each presumably as holy as the next. Once this armor was pierced by the simple question, Why?, it fell away, and all that was left was a collection of habits."[2]

Another way of looking at is: there are highly spiritual people in all religions; and there are nasty, hypocritical people in all religions. Therefore, belief systems must be completely beside the point. This is not to say that there's anything intrinsically wrong with belief. After all, magic has its beliefs too. Magicians, however, are aware that their beliefs are just a way of orienting themselves, not a description of what's really going on in the universe. The problem with belief lies in subscribing to a belief system which is based upon fear, particularly a fear as ridiculous as fear of death. The only real advantage magicians have over average people is that they no longer fear death. As a result, they're willing to take chances and risks that would paralyze average people with fear.

How do you overcome your fear of death? This is not a matter of bungee jumping, or going to war to prove your manhood, or forcing dire confrontations with death. Nor is it a matter of soothing yourself with beliefs about where you will go when you die. Rather, it is a matter of calm acceptance. Death is calm. It's being alive that's agitated and frenetic. Therefore, to overcome your fear of death, you have to make a conscious effort to calm yourself down in your day-to-day life. This means to just relax and let things unfold. It means to look squarely at your own sexual desires without freaking out, and just accept yourself as you are. It means to stop trying to make the people around you change, but just accept them as they are. It means to stop picking at things and fussing around generally. It means to stop struggling against the things you can't control.

I have a metaphor for this for my own life: breathing water. This comes from an article I once read in a scientific magazine about an experiment in which dogs and mice were put in cages which were then flooded with water that had been oxygenated so as to contain the same percentage of oxygen as air. As the cages filled up the animals freaked out and clawed frantically to try to escape. But then when they were covered with the water, they just settled down and relaxed and started breathing the water.

The way to find answers to life's problems is by calming down and just allowing the answers to come. And this includes death and fear of death. Whenever things seem out of control in your life, just tell yourself to relax and breathe the water. What else can you do?

Notes:

[1] *Luke* 16:22 – *"The poor man died and was carried by angels to Abraham's bosom. The rich man also died and was buried; and in Hades, being in torment, he lifted up his eyes and saw Abraham far off and Lazarus in his bosom ... "*

Luke 23:43 – (Jesus to thieves being crucified with him) *"Today you will be with me in Paradise."*

John 6:38-44 – *"I have come down from heaven, not to do my own will, but the will of him who sent me ... this is the will of my Father, that every one who sees the Son and believes in him should have eternal life; and I will raise him up at the last day."*

John 11:21-44 – (Resurrection of Lazarus)

I *Thessalonians* 4:13-17 – *"The Lord himself will descend from heaven with a cry of command, with the archangel's call, and with the sound of the trumpet of God. And the dead in Christ will rise first; then we who are alive, who are left, shall be caught up together with them in the clouds to meet the Lord in the air."*

[2] Rosten, Leo, *The Joys of Yiddish*, McGraw-Hill NYC 1968, page 491.

XII – Black Magicians and Vampires

I live in Guatemala, a country which is populated largely by Mayan Indians. There's a lot of magic going on, both white and black. Every little village in highland Guatemala has people who know a lot a lot more magic than I do; but they're not particularly writing books on the subject, much less in English.

As a result of all this attention, magic works pretty well in Guatemala. What a society emphasizes is what it tends to manifest. For example, material abundance works pretty well in the First World (at least for the moment), but not in Guatemala.

I have an American friend here who started out as a Mormon missionary with no belief in black magic. He married a Guatemalan woman and had children with her. Eventually the marriage dissolved, and this woman, bent on revenge, hired a black witch to curse my friend.

His car broke down frequently. Thieves ransacked his house several times when he was away. Payments due him were defaulted or stolen. Eventually he realized that all this bad luck wasn't a coincidence. He went to a witch himself to undo the spells his ex-wife's witch was casting. The witch did a long ritual, and at the end of it she told my friend that there was nothing she could do since his wife's witch was far more powerful than she was. Further, she didn't know anyone who could undo the curse.

It is not true, as the materialists would have you believe, that witchcraft only works on people who believe in it. On the contrary, it works on everyone; but materialists view as "coincidence" happenings which magicians view as cause and effect. Black magic is not essentially different from the selfishness, greed, bad faith, and lying which take place in our everyday society and relationships. All of our jealousy; bickering; people picking at each other; is inept black magic at work. All bad feelings are curses which do indeed cause the person they are directed at pain on some level.

What is Magic?

If you have ever returned home to find your place burglarized or vandalized, then you know that feeling of violation – like actually having been raped – which pervades the scene. You feel dirty and slimed-on. Magicians say that this feeling is a "light fiber" – like a curse – left by the burglar to suck your energy (your anger and fear at your own helplessness and vulnerability). Magicians believe that that is what the burglar was really after – not whatever it was he stole, but rather your anger and fear – which he can suck through the line he left there like soda through a straw.

In fact, these light fibers – which emerge from a person's navel and form an egg-shaped aura around the physical body – are visible to psychic people; that is to say, to people who are born with or have developed this faculty. See Barbara Brennan's book *Light Emerging*, which contains vivid drawings of what these lines look like to people with psychic vision. Carlos Castaneda's books also discuss light fibers at great length and detail, as does my book *Thought Forms*. The point is, that when we talk about vampires we're talking about everyday society: abusive parents, spouses, teachers, bosses, cops, airport officials; etc. Any bad faith; bullying; lying; sneakiness; even gossiping behind someone's back; is quite literally a vampirization of energy. Black magic is what everybody is doing to everyone else all the time, beneath a superficial veneer of social niceties.

Magicians say that the idea of other people's "webs" is no metaphor: that everybody is tied up with everyone else in the universe by fibers of light. In normal human relationships there is a give and take of energy (love) through these light fibers, which is what happens when people are making each other feel good. However, there are people who use these fibers only to take, not to give. These are the black magicians.

In point of fact, our entire society is based upon black magic and lying. When is the last time you told the truth about what you're really feeling and thinking inside to anyone? You can't tell the truth in our society about anything which matters – any talk except for vapid thought form persiflage is forbidden. Black magic is simply what everybody is doing to everybody else all the time underneath all the phoniness and tea party hypocrisy: everybody is just pretending that they're not doing it. However, there are some people who are just natural-born black magicians, just like some people are natural-born musicians or natural-born chefs. Natural born black magicians are very good at sucking other people's energy; and when they team up with demons, they can be superb.

In order to stay alive you must eat – devour other living beings. When you eat you destroy and assimilate the energy of other beings in order to maintain your own personal continuity. Thus, being alive in the world is, by its very nature, black magic. What is actually being consumed is not flesh but rather feelings.

You have been trained to believe that you live in a world of things; however, this is merely an appearance. In point of fact you live in a world of feelings. For example: when someone steals from you, or rips you off in some other way, what they are really after isn't your money, but rather your anger. Women are used to men coming onto them for sexual favors; and practically everyone has experienced hustlers coming onto them for money. However the actual gain when someone tries to force you to do something you don't want to do is not the sex or money, the surface payoff, but rather the bending you out of shape. It's your anger and fear that such people are after. By making you react they can suck your energy. Even a refusal, if made in anger or fear, is a positive payoff to such people.

People who are mooches or invade your space in some other way; who are gratuitously nasty, threatening, or annoying; who make you feel dirty, or used, or frazzled; are actually vampires who are out to suck your energy. If you react to them in any way at all, rather than brush them off non-reactively, then they got what they wanted from you.

There are certain people who are natural vampires. Just being around them is energy-depleting, and becoming involved in an intimate relationship with them can be devastating. We all know of couples where one partner emotionally trashes the other one, but the victim can't seem to separate, or even understand what is going on. This is because

What is Magic?

the vampire has his or her victim bewitched. Alcoholics and drug addicts often literally vampirize their families and friends. There are lots of families where one tyrannical dictator has everyone else in constant turmoil or jumping through hoops because of them: this person is literally sucking other family members' energy (and feeding it in turn to his or her demons).

All power struggles and bad faith are no different from what real vampires do. These activities are overseen and directed by demons, who get their little share of the vigorish. The difference between everyday space-jumpers and real vampires who can stay alive for centuries is a matter of degrees of competence. The mechanism is exactly the same. If there is any shame, compunction, or humanity there at all, then the person isn't yet a real vampire. All black magic takes shamelessness as its point of departure. Therefore, disordered personalities (lacking shame) make better black magicians than do neurotics (who are overburdened with shame). Black magicians are the living dead – psychopaths who succeed by killing off all of their humanity (their ability to feel); and who destroy other people without any compunction whatsoever – without even any sense that they are doing anything wrong; any more than you feel compunction about killing a mosquito.

Suppose someone presses you for something which you really don't feel like giving, but you do it anyway and then feel put out or used in the process. What actually happened was that the person shot a line (a light fiber) of desire into you and sucked your energy – your good feelings, your joy – through it like a straw. Practically everyone has experienced having had darts of black magic hurled at them, as when someone made you a gratuitous cutting, hurtful remark – or sent you an ugly, nasty look – which went straight to your heart and wounded you in your light fibers. The thought forms involved (the superficial, presenting events: the hurtful remarks or the nasty looks) are beside the point. What actually occurred in such moments is that the person threw a light fiber into your body (your solar plexus, heart, and head are the usual targets; sexual darts go in the genitals).

The basic principle involved in hurling darts of black magic is no different from that of hurling of darts of sexual turn-on, which pass between people when they look into each other's eyes and flash on each other sexually. At such moments one person (or both of them) hurl light fibers into the other person. The basic intent in both types of dart – sexual and hurtful – is the same: namely, to bind the other person with the light fibers attached to that dart, to be able to pass energy to and from that person. However, darts of black magic are obviously not voluntarily received (as are sexual and love darts, through which energy is given in an effort to make the person feel good). The object of black magic darts is to give nothing, but just to suck the other person's energy (good feelings) through these light fibers by making the person feel bad (fearful or angry).

Black magicians get a little lift of energy through the lines they have stuck in other people; but the main beneficiaries are their handlers, the demons who possess them and are sucking their energy in turn. It's like a chain of suckers: demons suck the black magicians, who have to keep finding victims to suck to keep their own energy up; and then the victims call in their own demons as a protection, and then they have to find victims of their own to suck.

Is it quite clear in this exposition that what we are talking about here is everyday society – everybody's relations with everyone around them: parents, teachers, bosses, coworkers, strangers in the supermarket? All this black magic is what's happening "beneath the surface" of everyday society, if you just open your eyes and *see* it.

A friend of mine who used to run the Iditarod dog sled race from Anchorage to Nome told me that when leaving rest stops it is necessary for dog sled teams to hide their departure intentions from other contestants, lest someone get on their trail shortly after they leave and "dog" them – follow in their track and pull themselves forward by sucking the energy of the leading team. My friend told me that it actually feels like having to drag someone behind you. This is similar to a technique my guidance taught me: when hiking in the country, try to place your footsteps on the receding footsteps of the person in front of you. Not only is this a great exercise in maintaining concentration (if you aren't paying complete attention to the person's feet, you lose the thread entirely) but also you pick up energy from that person.

What makes this subject so difficult to understand is that there is nothing visible going on, nothing you can point to openly. Vampirization, like bewitching, takes place on a feeling level. To the victim the feelings are as palpable as being physically attacked – physically slimed on. In fact these lines are visible to psychic people – that is to say, to people who are born with or have developed this faculty. See Barbara Brennan's book *Light Emerging*[1] for drawings of what these lines look like to a person with psychic vision. The only way to avoid being vampirized in such a situation is to not react at all. To refuse the vampire in anger, for example, or to recoil in disgust, is as much a gain for the vampire as acceding to him is. However, the light fibers which a vampire has in his victims are themselves irritating, like mosquito bites. It is difficult for the victims who have such lines in them not to react to the vampire's provocations (by constantly thinking about him).

This is an important point: all "you" really are is your attention – where you are placing your attention right this moment. That's all you are, and that's all you have. What demons and vampires (and the people who love you as well) try to do is to capture your moment-to-moment attention by making you feel fearful or angry (or happy, in the case of the people who love you). The only way to unplug those light fibers is to completely ignore the provocation: to cease all thoughts and feelings about the vampire – to just stop caring about him and his antics. Obviously, this ultimately requires the loss of a considerable amount of self-pity on your part since it is the victim's self-pity which encourages and engages a vampire's invasion of the victim's space. Vampires can only get into your space if you let them in. But, to muster the necessary ruthlessness to cast them out, you must rid yourself of your use of the vampire as an excuse to pity yourself (by being afraid of him or angry at him). The ritual of cutting and casting out these lines (described below) is a good place to start, symbolizing as it does the definitive intent to cut that vampire from your life.

When I broke up with my girlfriend F., I did so in such an abrupt and unexpected manner that it surprised even me (it was as if something welled up in me and cried "ENOUGH!"). I learned later from her that after this breakup a wound opened on her left breast that suppurated for months. Anyway, for about six months after this breakup I was not my usual, heavy, mopey self: on the contrary, I felt an unwonted lightness of spirit – happy, optimistic, joyous. And then I came down into my usual dull self. I asked my spirit guides what that was all about, and they told me that for the preceding six months – since the breakup – I had been vampirizing F.'s energy, as she had been doing to me theretofore; that I had turned the equation around and used the lines that joined us to suck from her instead of permitting her to suck from me. And that when I came down six months later, she must have done something from her side to put a stop to it.

When my guides told me that, I suddenly understood F. (and my ex-wife) better. I had always supposed that on some level these women knew what they were doing to me – trashing me emotionally – but they just refused to acknowledge it. However, after I, myself, did the same thing to F. unwittingly – I realized that the women hadn't known consciously that they were vampirizing my energy and causing me great pain. All they knew was that they would be happy and joyous and minding their own business; and then all of a sudden I would appear and start screaming at them for no reason whatsoever. It wasn't until I found myself on the sucking side of the vampire equation for the first (and only) time in my life that I understood that most everyday vampires don't have a conscious clue as to what they are doing. But that doesn't mean they're not doing it.

The subject of magic is so very difficult to understand – indeed, it defies understanding. As a mathematician, I rather like explanations and causality; being able to see mechanisms involved; and so on. But magic doesn't work that way. There is only intent. I used to beseech my guides over and over to explain to me, "HOW does she do it?" But now they answer me, "The same way you did it to F." And I have no idea how I did it that time – I couldn't repeat it at will; I didn't even know that I was doing it at the time. At this point in my magical training I know that there are no mechanisms involved; neither are there procedures. Magical events are caused by intending them; or better said, by awaiting them – there's no step-by-step modus operandi.[2] And that intending can take place on a subconscious level. Indeed, the practice of magic is merely a matter of making that which most people do unconsciously, conscious. Becoming a magician is simply a matter of learning to look at everyday life the way it actually is, without all the hypocrisy and stupidity.

The difference between black and white magic is that in black magic emotions are repressed, whereas in white magic emotions are felt but not acted upon. White magic requires true discipline, whereas black magic is based ultimately upon fear and anger. White magic seeks to diminish self-importance, whereas black magic seeks to increase it. In black magic the practitioner jumps deeply into other people's space; whereas in white magic the idea is to keep out of other people's space. What both black and white magic have in common is ruthless ejection of other people from your own space.

As mentioned previously, people can only enter your space if you let them enter it. The way you let them enter is by thinking about them and reacting to them emotionally: caring what they do or don't do. To eject them from your space is a matter of ceasing to think about them. You free yourself from them when you stop caring about them, when you stop fawning or feeling offended by them, when you stop rehearsing mental scenarios of validation or vindication or vengeance. In other words, the trick to both white and black magic is to have conscious, volitional control over your moment-to-moment thoughts and desires. That's the only way you can ultimately disentangle yourself from other people's webs of black magic.

There are lots of spiritual paths which aim at the cessation of thoughts and desires. Usually a spiritual path aims at control of either one or the other of these, since to quiet our restless minds necessarily quiets down our relentless desires, and vice versa. The aspirant merely chooses a path which suits his or her own temperament. Where I'd characterize Buddhism as a path of stilling thought, the path of magic is a path of stilling desire. The black magicians and vampires you run into in your everyday life are terrific teachers in the craft of stilling desire – namely the desire to up and smack 'em one.

A fundamental principle of magic, both black and white, is being completely non-reactive emotionally; not permitting any dart of desire to escape. The white magician relaxes into a state of indifference, whereas the black magician clenches up into a state of heightened tension. The white magician reaches towards a state of mind in which nothing is important, whereas the black magician induces a state of mind in which his lower self is the most important thing in the universe. The goals are different, but the technique of getting there is the same in either case: holding all desire inside instead of frittering it away in self-pity.

One trick I've found that works in black magic situations is to say to yourself, "What this person is really after is my anger, to reflect his own self-hatred back at him. If I give it to him, he wins! I can't let him get away with that!" Or else tell yourself, "I'm not going to feed this guy's demons!" And then laugh it off; or at least try to as best you can. When they actually throw a dart into your light fibers, you can't help but react. But then you try to shake it off (literally) instead of nursing a grievance.

Another helpful technique is to take an objective look at the person who is hassling you and see why they are doing it (from their own point of view), to get an understanding (if not sympathy) for the person. When you see how pitiful most of your enemies truly are, it makes you less interested in wasting your energy thinking about them or reacting to them.

The times I've reached my higher self in normal, everyday (not psychedelic-induced) consciousness was when my enemies pushed me there (to the Place of No Pity[3]) by driving me beyond the limits of endurance. My enemies are the best friends I've had on the spiritual path; and this is not

What is Magic?

just one of those trite spiritual homilies – I really mean it. I couldn't have gotten to where I've gotten to (including a first-hand understanding of what demons really are and how to cast them out; what curses are and how to undo them; as well as how vampires operate and how to fend them off) without the thorough and relentless tutelage of my enemies.

Another thing that helps me is my knowledge from experience that most of the time when someone rips me off for something, whatever he ripped off is something I'm better off without. Or sometimes the rip-off gives me a whole new slant on something completely different. In other words, I try to take a detached view, and figure out what the lesson here is. It's a form of deliberately tricking yourself. This doesn't always work in the moment, of course, but with practice it's possible to detach yourself from the vampires instead of acceding to them. Another technique you can use when someone lays a bad vibe on you is to jump up and down and shake your arms and body and head to shake their bad vibes off of you. Also, resorting to nature spirits every day for an hour or so is the easiest and pleasantest way to intend your obsessive thoughts and moods instead of being slave to them.

All victims are willing victims. All victims are indulging themselves in self-pity: that's their payoff. To try to force other people to change is to do black magic to them. To expect or hope that other people will change is to make yourself a black magician's willing victim. Let them make their own decisions; it's really none of your damn business, you know. And only by being indifferent can you disentangle yourself from their webs.

According to my guides and Carlos Castaneda,[4] vampires who can stay alive for centuries most certainly do exist (though I've never met one personally). They start out like everyday black magicians, and have the help of demons to guide them. However the popular conception of them, such as Ann Rice's books, is way off base. Vampires are not sensitive, artistic, misunderstood beings who engage in soul-searching and wistfulness. They are total scumbags. They don't bite people in the neck. They just scare them to death and thereby absorb their power. They draw sustenance from their victims' fear. Vampires and black magicians don't kill people: they get people to kill themselves.

Black magic is basically the same thing that a torturer or sadist does. However, by getting a quick emotional charge out of his victim's fear, the torturer or sadist immediately wastes the energy he is drawing from his victim. To be a successful vampire, the black magician must not only repress all shame, as the torturer does, but also all feelings of satiation. The torturer or sadist hates his victim and thus dissipates the victim's fear energy with his hatred (actually he fears his victim, his victim's vulnerability, and the hatred is a cover of shamelessness to deny his fear of his own vulnerability).

A true vampire doesn't indulge in expressing any feelings whatsoever. To him, it's just a snack. Real vampires don't waste time or energy in gloating. They step on people like most people step on bugs, without a thought. Their power comes from rigid control over their emotions: holding everything in. Vampires stifle all human feelings, all joy, compassion, and love. They give themselves wholly over to their own importance.

The next level down on the incompetence scale below the torturer or sadist is the everyday, garden variety son of a bitch whom we all know. The difference between the torturer or sadist and the common S.O.B. is that the S.O.B. uses his hatred to stoke his self-pity. Isn't it true that most S.O.B.'s think that they are the ones being imposed upon? This contrasts with the torturer or sadist who, like the vampire, is pitiless. Self-pity is a dangerous stand since it is a thin mask for shame.

If you're going to indulge in black magic, then you have to be completely shameless about it, as torturers and vampires are. That's the only way to win at the black magic game. You have to consciously acknowledge what you're doing; consciously choose evil and take responsibility for doing evil.

What common S.O.B.'s do is commit evil and pretend that they aren't doing it. Usually such people put on a mask of self-righteous justification, such as a thought form that they are "helping" the other person. Everyday S.O.B.'s repress shame instead of acknowledging and flaunting it. This is a

What is Magic?

losing set-up. To commit evil, to deliberately bend other people out of shape and not cop to what you're doing, only works as long as the victims accede to it. If the victims detach themselves from S.O.B.'s by deliberately ignoring them and their goads rather than reacting in fear or anger, then the S.O.B.'s are doomed. Shame will ultimately out.

So, how do you disentangle yourself from a black magician who's got you trapped and is vampirizing your energy, such as an abusive parent, spouse, teacher, boss; or, as happened to my friend, a bona fide witch? You have to stop thinking and caring about them. However, this is well-nigh impossible until you detach the light fibers they've stuck in you, through which they are sucking your energy. Having other people's lines in you is irritating and depletes your energy by making you think constantly about them. Detaching these lines of black magic through visualization is an easy way to begin the disentanglement process.

Pulling out lines is not difficult to do, but it is easiest if you are being directed by your spirit guides. Complete instructions for pulling black magicians' lines out of yourself are given in my book *Thought Forms*. As a stopgap, try this: take a firm stance, and imagine you are gripping with both hands a rope or cord stuck in your navel. This is the usual place where black magicians stick such lines in your body. If additionally you feel hypnotized by and unable to separate from the sexual relationship, then the person probably also stuck lines in your genitals. If there's a lot of hatred underlying the relationship, particularly accompanied by health or financial problems, then the person probably has lines in your head. You have to cast a little spell of banishment for each line the black magician has in your body.

Try to actually feel or imagine something like a rope in your hands which goes from the respective part of your body to the other person, through which they are sucking energy from you. You can look at a photograph of the person who is vampirizing you while you do this, or just visualize him or her standing there before you.

Then, with a movement of great repugnance, determination, and finality, jerk the line out of your body and cast it to the ground. You don't have to actually see the light fiber (though some sensitive people do) as long as you can feel it – i.e., imagine it is there.

If that person was really bringing you down, you should feel immediate relief and release after doing this exercise. Sometimes you don't even realize the extent to which they were bringing you down until you get their damn lines out of you. You should feel more youthful, since that's what black magicians vampirize: other people's youthfulness and joy. The next time you meet that person you'll be surprised by how different you feel about them, and by how much clearer your understanding of the dynamics of the relationship is. You'll have much more detachment and freedom from this person. It is by getting control over yourself, by being decisive rather than self-pitying, that you can take control of any relationship.

Notes:

[1] Brennan, Barbara, *Light Emerging*, Bantam NYC 1993.

[2] It is true that some magical operations – such as spirit invocations – do have strict procedures; but this is more to please the spirits than intrinsically necessary to make the magic work. I, personally, eschew a lot of ritual, fancy clothes, formulaic incantations, etc. unless these have been mandated by the spirits involved themselves. This sort of claptrap is just a matter of taste, it has nothing to do with making magic work; whereas intent has everything to do with it.

[3] See "The Place of No Pity" chapters in Carlos Castaneda's *The Power of Silence* and my book *Bob Makransky Tells It Like It Is!*

[4] See the "Death Defiers" chapter in Carlos Castaneda's *The Fire From Within*.

XIII – Power Places

There are certain places on earth which radiate positive or negative energy, and these are called power places. I can recognize when I'm at such a place because I invariably hear a whistling-like sound in my head – a sound which is more felt than heard. If the place is really powerful, I also feel a pressure in my sinuses, and the more powerful the place is, the greater the pressure. However, these sensations are peculiar to me.

Everyone reacts to power places differently. Some people don't feel anything out of the ordinary at such places. Sometimes they think I'm putting them on when I say we're at a power place. I believe, however, that anyone can train him or herself to feel these kinds of vibrations. Hugging trees is a good place to start your training. Pick out big trees and hug them until you can start to differentiate the different energies coming out of different trees. It's subtle at first, what you're supposed to feel, but after a while you get the idea. Once you can pick up trees' vibrations, it's an easy matter to pick up the vibrations emanating from power spots.

It's easiest to find power spots when you are in enhanced awareness (see the "Following Feelings" chapter of my book *Magical Living* for details). In fact, this is the only way to find them, although you can sometimes make an educated guess in normal awareness, based on how a place looks. In enhanced awareness you can *feel* what's going on; so you are guided to them.

"How do I know if this place is really a power spot?" is as difficult a question to answer as "How do I know if I'm really in love?" No one can feel your feelings but you. You have to be willing to rely upon your own intuition and intent as a guidance system instead of your thinking. Then the earth herself starts talking to you.

Churches; especially old churches; especially old churches erected on sites of previous pagan worship, are often built on power spots. Public parks are often built around power spots.

Everyone is innately attuned to power spots on the earth. This knowledge is our inheritance as human beings from our hunter / gatherer forebears. All humans intuitively align themselves with the earth's energy, like iron filings to a magnet. People naturally do this, whether consciously or not. Unfortunately the busyness of everyday routines and necessities tends to blot out most people's innate ability to tune into the subtle energies surrounding them. Therefore most people perforce obey this natural law unconsciously.

Magicians consciously utilize power spots to accomplish their aims. All people receive boosts of energy, or else are debilitated, at these places. Power spots out in nature are often recognizable by their striking physical features, beyond the vibrations which they emit. Spirits often take up abode at power spots too. If you feel a personality such as male or female, young or old, jolly or somber, at a power spot, that's the spirit residing at the place, not the spot itself. Power spots are just energy replenishing or energy depleting, as the case may be. They're not alive.

Carlos Castaneda's teacher don Juan pointed out that people intuitively seek out energy-replenishing power spots to pause for a rest. Along a footpath, for example, they get tired and sit down for a while at an energy-replenishing power spot, but they hurry along quickly past an energy-depleting power spot.

Power spots are either / or propositions – either they help you or they hurt you. All power spots tend to concentrate and magnify whatever mood you are in, which is why it's best to be mentally empty and in a light mood when you go to them. Moreover, power spots can become obsessing. Depleting power spots concentrate and magnify your bad moods, such as anger, lust, or depression.

Particularly when you go to one on an empty stomach, being on a power spot gives a physical sensation like an abstract or mental orgasm. It's a stimulating feeling, felt more in the spine and head than in the genitals. It's a feeling of power. Therefore, if you find yourself getting angry or into self-glorifying fantasies, leave immediately and don't return for a while.

What is Magic?

Don't get into fantasizing of any sort. Don't think about other people, or think at all. Listen to sounds and clear your mind until you feel the power directly, not symbolically in terms of thoughts of grandiosity or sexual turn-on. Don't go to power spots to pull yourself out of moods you shouldn't be feeling in the first place, such as self-pity or self-righteousness. The power spot will just magnify that mood.

On the other hand, there are no better places to heal yourself and to grow spiritually than power spots. Power spots are used to relax yourself, to relieve tension, to get in touch with your true feelings. At power spots you can find peace and tranquility. If you're having an argument with someone and want to find a *modus vivendi* and peace, take them to a power spot – especially during a relevant planetary hour – to talk it over.

Just because a place looks scary or forbidding doesn't mean that it's evil. All that means is that it's powerful. In fact, the more powerful a place is, usually the scarier it looks. When you get on it, or in it, however, it should make you feel relaxed, calm, and floating. A truly evil place, on the contrary, feels nervous, agitated, and disorienting. Evil spots give you the willies: you wouldn't go near them in the dark on a bet.

It's good to go out to power spots, or big trees, every day for half an hour or so at minimum just to relax and replenish. I've done this daily for the past twenty-five years. Indeed, this has been my main spiritual practice. It calms me down, makes me feel more peaceful and contented generally. Also it helps me get over specific hassles in my current affairs. When I feel disappointed or hurt by something that has happened and want to get over it, I go to a power spot or power tree, or to my little water spirit, who lives at a power place.

There are general power spots which work for everyone. There are also individual power spots. The general spots are places where the earth's light fibers, sometimes called ley lines, cross or agglomerate. Individual power spots are special to particular individuals, and have no power for anyone else. They're usually not as striking to the eye as general power spots, which can be quite dramatic in appearance.

Individual power spots are places where the person's light fibers join the earth. They can be likened to the person's roots. It is through your fibers joined to the earth that the earth sends you her loving, healing energy, without which you would be in really bad shape. Going to your individual power spot is like going directly to the tap. The pressure of the earth's love for you is a bit stronger at these places. You should go to them just prior to embarking on a journey, doing an important ritual, asking for a raise; any time you need a boost of vitality and clarity.

Besides the fact that some places have more powerful vibrations than others, for good or evil, it is indubitable that psychic phenomena happen more in some places than in others. These phenomena occur more in places where people accept and expect such things.

I've had lots of psychic experiences since I moved to Guatemala, whereas that sort of thing never happened when I lived in the U.S. In the U.S. people expect that science will keep coming up with miracles, so in the U.S. science keeps coming up with miracles. But nobody expects great scientific breakthroughs in Guatemala, so those things don't happen there.

On the other hand, people in Guatemala take psychic phenomena as the norm, so psychic phenomena are more prevalent there, both amongst the Mayan Indians and the Spanish-descent *ladinos*. I've seen wealthy, high-society *ladina* women in high heels and expensive jewelry bowing down and making petitions before the Mayan idol San Simon. And it's common for people who have never had an ESP experience in their entire lives to have one happen to them on their first visit to Guatemala. When one of my neighbors died, her ghost was seen a few days later by a Peace Corps volunteer visitor who, up until that moment, had never believed in ghosts.

The Call of the Pagan Gods

Just as our modern cities are basically designed as places of commerce, ancient cities built by spiritual civilizations were designed as places of pilgrimage. Our society today is run by the media, government, business, academia, and organized religion. Older societies, by contrast, were directed by spirits. The whole purpose of ceremonial centers – the cities of old – was to induce altered states of consciousness. This is the purpose of all shamanic rituals, but ceremonial centers were especially designed to do this.

Today's archeologists are the reincarnated priests of the gods of old. They are reconstructing their ancient ceremonial centers in this lifetime, although in most cases they are doing this unconsciously. How do you suppose Schliemann found Troy? He was there in a previous incarnation. That's how he knew where Troy was, and where the gold was buried. Archeologists are the ones who discover these sites at the behest of their ancient gods from previous lifetimes.

The tourists who are called to visit these sites enter altered states of consciousness, to the extent that they permit this. At the very least they are acted upon by the ancient gods who inhabit those sites. We neo-pagans who do special rituals to invoke ancient gods at these power places are just making a formal gesture, a conscious acknowledgement, of what everyone who goes to these places does there anyway.

The old pagan gods are being heard once more. The old pagan gods are slouching towards Bethlehem to be born, and they shall be heard and obeyed once again. The pagan gods sometimes seem to present an angry aspect, like Jehovah in the Old Testament, but I don't find them angry at all. They are, however, extremely punctilious in demanding respect. You don't mess around with them, or treat them disrespectfully. If you do, you will be very, very sorry. It's best to acknowledge them and treat them with the respect that they deserve.

The ancient gods, working primarily through restored power places, are trying to save the earth. Indeed, they are perhaps our only hope, since all our modern human institutions are failing miserably.

If you ever have the opportunity to visit one of these ancient temples, remember that the old spirits who inhabited these sites in ancient days are still there and want to talk to you. If you are a person on the spiritual path with no particular direction yet, a visit to such a power place, particularly one to which you feel drawn, would be a good starting point. If you are attracted to a certain place, it probably means that you had a past life there.

Go there, take a little gift to the spirits of the place such as a pretty flower or stone, or something you've made yourself. Ask the spirits of the place to give you a lesson and help you find your spiritual path. You'll get the answer you're looking for. It's guaranteed.

XIV – The Magician's God

The magician's conception of God is very different from the Judeo-Christian-Islamic conception. This is not to say that one is right and the other is wrong. On the contrary, a tenet of magic is that what is really going on out there in the universe is not anything the human mind can possibly conceive of. Therefore all conceptions (beliefs) are wrong. Indeed, a human conception of God, no matter what it is, has definitely got to be puny in comparison with whatever God really is.

However it is instructive to compare the two conceptions of God since the two versions have different implications for how we should behave in our everyday lives. Emulating God, becoming more Godlike, is the meat and bone of any spiritual practice. How we conceive of God will determine what our spiritual ideal is, and what we are trying to accomplish in our spiritual lives.

To avoid confusion, we'll refer to the Judeo-Christian-Islamic supreme deity as "God", and to the magicians' supreme deity as "the Spirit".

Most people believe that God cares about them personally. Conventional religions inculcate fear of death, and then teach people to cover over that fear of death with the promise of heaven. People believe that if they do X and Y and Z, then God will be pleased with them and they will go to heaven when they die.

The magician's path is very different. Magicians know that death is not only inevitable, but is nothing to fear. Death is right there in the background all the time. Magicians learn to feel that they are in the presence of death every minute. There is no miraculous salvation. Anything that comes through for them they are going to have to make happen themselves, since the Spirit doesn't care a rat's butt about them one way or the other. Use your head: if God cared about you, would He have condemned you to death? Believing that you're special to God is the acme of self-pity.

Both God and the Spirit are all-powerful and created the universe intentionally. That is to say, creation was no accident, as the materialists would have it.¹ However the Judeo-Christian-Islamic God is monotheistic: God stands outside of His creation. The Spirit, on the other hand, is pantheistic: the Spirit is everything and everything is the Spirit.

God cares about His creation: "God so loved the world that He gave His only begotten son … ." The Spirit, on the other hand, is utterly detached and indifferent, so that there is no point in worshipping it or praying to it: "The Spirit was so indifferent to the world that it left all sentient beings to figure things out for themselves." As Taisha Abelar put it, "Seers who have gazed at the boundless have attested that the boundless stares back with a cold, unyielding indifference."

Since spiritual practice entails emulating the supreme deity, evidently caring is a fundamental part of Judeo-Christian-Islamic practice, whereas being detached and indifferent is essential to magic. Most people need the sense of security (from the magicians' viewpoint, false sense of security) of believing that God is concerned about them personally. They need to feel that they fit in and belong somewhere. They must believe that they're not all alone, at the mercy of ineffable, incomprehensible, and wholly impersonal forces of the universe. However, magicians need no such assurance. Indeed, they find such a belief useless baggage which weighs them down.

We all lie to ourselves constantly. For example, we believe that our luck is going to change really soon; or that this person we're in love with is the most marvelous person on earth; and so on. Really, lying to ourselves is about the only way we can keep on keeping on much of the time. The difference between magicians and most people is that magicians know that they are lying to themselves. An example of a magician's lie is "you create your own reality." This is something magicians have to believe, even though they know it's a lie.² Magicians choose their lies with care. Thus their conception of what the Spirit is, is another carefully crafted lie.

Although the Spirit is too vast to have what might be termed a personality, nonetheless it is correct to say that the Spirit is a trickster. The Spirit is a trickster because the

What is Magic?

magician's reality is a reality of trickery, and you create your own reality and your own deity with it.

Magicians have to trick themselves to stay on the magician's path, else who in blazes would follow it? Magic is a path of utmost responsibility, self-discipline and self-denial. Magic requires being utterly alone and facing up to the truth. No one wants to take responsibility or face the truth; not even magicians. Somehow or other they have to be tricked into it.

The Spirit is a trickster because although it will bring you what you want, what you've been praying for all along, it usually does this in such a guise that you don't recognize it for what it is, and you therefore reject it. As an example, more than once I've seen the Spirit bring a person a true soul mate when they were on the rebound from a break-up, and still too filled with self-pity to see that this person they met "accidentally" was the one they were praying for all along.

How many times have I seen the Spirit bring someone their true heart's desire on a silver platter, yet the person rejected it because they still had too much self-hatred to permit themselves to feel happiness. What keeps you from seeing and grasping the Spirit's gifts is your own self-pity, which blinds you to everything except how much you're suffering.

My spirit guides used trickery as their main teaching tool. Now that I'm more or less on my own, I have to trick myself. For many years I fantasized that one day a beautiful woman would come into my life and love me and make me happy. My spirit guides really seized on that one. Every time a likely woman came across my horizon they played it to the hilt: "Oh yes! She's the one you've been waiting for, definitely! Very soon now all your dreams will come true and you'll find true love!" They encouraged me to make an ass of myself and follow every mirage until it too turned to dust. And in my stupidity and desperation I fell for that ploy every time, even long after I understand intellectually what they were doing and why. They were trying to burn that expectation out of me via exhaustion. They always told me that spiritual growth is mostly a matter of exhaustion, of giving up one's own will. They were right, but I'm so stubborn and obsessive that it took me a long, long time to burn out. Now that their tricks don't work on me anymore, I have to trick myself. This is what the technique of Creative Visualization is all about.

The point is that the magician's deity is a trickster because the magician's path is a path of trickery. There is no ultimate truth in this. The Christian and Hindu Gods are gods of love because these paths are devotional paths. Magic, by contrast, is a very rational path – detached and coldly objective. There's love in it, of course, and joy. Lots of joy, actually. In fact, the joy – the incredible joy – is the only excuse for following the magician's path, because otherwise it's too daunting. But the principle mainspring to action is *intent*. What drives magicians forward is the quest for power and freedom.

Although the Spirit is wholly impersonal and indifferent, it nonetheless can be put to use. From the magical point of view, the Spirit is your servant. Every time you desire something, no matter how trivial, you emit an order, a desire line. Desire lines are actual fibers of light which pop out of your navel. They can be considered commands to the Spirit, who starts racing around trying to fulfill your order.

The reason why most people can't bring their desires to realization is because they have their desire lines tangled up. They don't really want things to spring into existence the moment they think of them, as happens in dreams. Most people are afraid of taking responsibility for that much power. They would prefer to pretend that they don't have that much potential control over their own lives and destinies. They prefer to cringe helplessly and wallow in self-pity rather than take on the awesome responsibility of total control over themselves: control over their moment-to-moment thoughts, feelings, and actions.

Most people prefer to believe in fantasies, like that some day God is going to bring them exactly what they desire, with no effort on their part. This is why they need to believe in a God who is outside of themselves, disconnected from them, rather than that they are the Spirit, and whatever situation they find themselves in is their own creation. To change it they're going to have to change themselves by changing their way of looking at the situation they are in. Average people don't want to have to do this.

The Abrahamic God pities you and thus mirrors your own self-pity. The Spirit, on the other hand, is pitiless and can only be commanded by erasing self-pity. Power comes from taking responsibility for your decisions. In particular, this means taking responsibility for the situation in which you find yourself in the present moment – dealing with the reality of it instead of wishing it would go away.

Taking responsibility means not blaming other people or the Spirit for your own unhappiness, nor trying to slough off your unhappiness on other people around you. Rather, it means understanding that you have deliberately, if unconsciously, chosen the circumstances of your life, and only you can change them. When you truly understand this in your heart, when you resign yourself to this truth and begin to act on it, then you become one with the Spirit.

Notes:

[1] Even materialistic science has its God concepts. In mathematics it's called The Axiom of Choice; in biology, Natural Selection; in classical physics, The Second Law of Thermodynamics; in quantum physics, Probability. Any intellectual system which purports to describe the workings of the universe must needs have a decision-making mechanism – a representation of intent.

[2] It's a lie because it's an intellectual construct, and all intellectual constructs (beliefs) are lies. What's really going on out there in the universe is completely random, as the Buddhists and quantum physicists assure us. We *don't* create our own realities. The usefulness of this particular lie consists in providing a point of reference around which intent can be rallied. Therefore it is a more functional lie for a magician than the belief in going to heaven. The belief in heaven tends to inflate self-pity – glory thought forms such as complacency, self-satisfaction and arrogance – and thereby dissipates intent. To magicians only intent matters, not belief systems or being "right."

XV – Magical Time

There are magical moments when your importance and familiarity are lessened, and you step out of normal life and enter the world of magic. Psychedelic plants and drugs can do this. Spirits can also do this. For example, new converts to any religion frequently experience a temporary high induced by the spirits of that religion.

Sometimes magical moments just happen by themselves when the time is right. Omens and portents come to you in magical time. The "Following Feelings" chapter of my book *Magical Living* explains how to shift into magical time deliberately. Here I'll just describe what I mean by the term "magical time."

In magical time, to a greater or lesser degree, you step into the world of dreams while still awake. What you consider being awake is actually a specialized form of dreaming. What keeps you awake is the feeling that things are important to you and familiar to you. Importance and familiarity are like screens through which you filter your waking experience to make it more stable and persistent than dreaming. Importance and familiarity enable you to focus your attention and make sense of things. At the same time they make your life predictable and boring.

The goal of magic is to lower your importance and familiarity enough so that the world once again becomes as bright and new as it is to an infant. To do this requires a shift in the way that you focus your attention. Instead of relying upon thought as a spur to action, magicians rely upon intent: gut-level intuition, direct knowing. They read the signs of the time. They wait upon omens and portents before acting.

Omens are the way the Spirit speaks to you. Manifestations of the Spirit are indicated by omens. Similarly, any declaration of your own to the Spirit must be preceded by a vocalized statement of intent. This is what praying and casting spells are all about. It's rather like the formality of signing your name to a contract. These are all symbolic acts, and what is being symbolized is *irrevocability*.

What is Magic?

The Spirit uses omens to remind you of its presence: to warn you of danger, to sign that you are on the right track, or simply to fill you with awe. The Spirit sends you omens to reassure you, to let you know that it's there in the background, and to move you into magical time.

Omens can be recognized by their emotional content. To a noninvolved bystander they appear to be only coincidences. An omen only has meaning for the one to whom the Spirit is manifesting. For example, the outbreak of the American Civil War was heralded by the appearance of a very bright comet. Of course, this comet appeared all over the world. Some commentators would argue, therefore, that this can't be taken as an omen for any particular country. However the comet was only an omen to Americans because it only had emotional meaning to Americans. The Americans at that time understood very well what it meant. The New York *Herald* wrote then that the comet frightened the common people "who regard it with fear, looking upon it as something terrible, bringing in its train wars and desolation".

Omens are final. Pronouncements of individual spirits may be literally true or not, but omens are pronouncements of the Spirit itself. Omens come from the source, and they are irrevocable. Often an omen has occurred in my life whose meaning was obvious but I didn't want to accept the truth of it; but omens are always true. For example, I wear charms on a necklace which have a symbolic meaning to me. Any time that necklace has broken it has been an omen that I really messed up, or that I was on the brink of messing up, that which my charms symbolize.

My totem animal is the eagle. Since there are very few eagles where I live, my guides have told me that large hawks can also serve as messengers for me. They told me that whenever I see a large hawk I should watch it until it disappears, and note the direction in which it disappears. That direction will often have a symbolic meaning.

In my own case, for example, the southwest is my joy direction. Guatemala, where I live now, is southwest of Philadelphia, where I was born and brought up. Lake Atitlan, where I've had some truly magical experiences, is southwest of my present home. My water spirit, where I go to wash off bad moods, is southwest of my house. So, if I see a large hawk disappear to the southwest I know something joyous is indicated or will happen.

However, not every large hawk that I see is an omen. I asked my guides how to tell when a hawk, or any other singular occurrence, is an omen, as opposed to just a coincidence. How can you tell if a dream is prophetic or significant rather than just a dream? They replied that you have to feel it, to listen with your heart; and then you'll know when something is an omen, or when a dream is prophetic. Sometimes I am able to do this. When I know in my heart that something is an omen or that a certain dream is prophetic, I also know intuitively what that omen or dream means.

When the Spirit is really serious about giving a message, the omens will appear in groups of three. Otherwise, if I'm not sure whether something was an omen or not, I ask my spirit guides to interpret the omen or dream for me.

Omens are happening for everyone all the time, but most people are too busy running hither and thither to pay attention to them. This is what becoming a magician is all about: slowing down. Magical time is considerably slower than hustle-bustle time.

I was once in love with a woman in magical time. At the behest of my patron spirits, at a particularly low point in my life, I journeyed to the shores of Lake Atitlan. I hung out for a few weeks in the village of Panajachel selling horoscopes to tourists on the street. My spirits were in charge of this trip. As spirits can sometimes do, they lowered my importance and familiarity so that I shifted into magical time for my entire stay.

I had been given to understand that I would find true love on this trip. The spirits had me doing moment-to-moment Creative Visualizations of this possibility from the day I arrived. And when I met C. they told me, "She's the one."

I made no overt moves but continued the continuous Creative Visualizations with her, rather than an abstract female, as the object. And at a certain moment, sitting around

What is Magic?

a hotel room on a rainy day with her and several other people, she and I happened to look into one another's eyes and ... .

The climax of the entire affair (or non-affair, as it turned out) was a party to which I went, expecting her to be there. While she wasn't there physically, I could feel her presence there beside me the whole time. My spirits later explained this sensation to me as follows:

Spirits: "What keeps you glued into one track or lifetime is the sense of familiarity. To break that track is to feel all your lifetimes and probable realities at once, just like you felt C.'s presence at that party in another probable reality. That's an example of how you can have two different memories of the same event: going to the party with C., and going to the same party without her."

Me: "Did the same things happen at both parties?"

Spirits: "Yes. Eduardo sang at both parties, but not the same songs. What do you think, stupid? Of course different things happened at both parties. That's not the point. The point is that life consists of feelings. You can only get to those feelings directly by getting past the screen of thought forms of importance and familiarity that hide them. There was a feeling at that party. Remember when you suddenly felt that you had to return immediately, and you jumped up and raced out of the party without even saying goodbye to anyone, and when you got to the pier – by a weird turn of events – you missed the last boat back to Panajachel? And the next day you learned that it was at that precise moment that C. had left for Mexico?"

Me: "How will I ever forget it?"

Spirits: "You were dreaming then, you know. That event didn't occur in normal, waking consciousness. Or rather, it did, but it didn't. Does that explain it? You know that things like what happened to you that day don't occur in real life. They only occur in dreams. You were dreaming that day. That's what your everyday life would be like if you weren't pegging it down to familiarity.

"What makes the world of waking consciousness a drab, dull place is familiarity. Familiarity breeds contempt. That is a true statement. Familiarity is a way of grabbing onto the world, of grabbing onto other people, of clinging to them and bringing them down. Familiarity is a bringdown.

"Just as lucid dreaming is a state in which things are separated, but there is no (or minimal) importance, so too is lucid dreaming a state in which things are known, or recognizable, but are thoroughly unfamiliar. To remove the familiarity from everyday life is to enter into the state of lucid dreaming, just as you did at that party.

"Getting rid of familiarity is getting rid of control. You can only control things – your environment, other people – by making them familiar. Making things familiar is to control them. Your question about e.g. Nazis controlling Jews by forcing them into a nightmare, into a situation in which they had no control, doesn't contravene the theory. It reinforces it.

"The waking state is controllable only as long as it seems familiar. The trick, then, is to be quite comfortable with everything out of control, as it were. When things are out of control, are unfamiliar, then you are dreaming. The more out of control you let your daily life be, the more you are actually dreaming rather than being awake. And that's when you step into magical time."

What is Magic?

XVI – Magic and Morality

Is magic immoral? For that matter, are masturbation, pre- and extra-marital sex, insider trading on the stock market, immoral? Society says that these things are immoral. However, everybody does them, and everybody's always done them. Because they're supposedly immoral, people just pretend that they aren't doing them, or else hide the fact that they're doing them.

Is manipulating other people immoral? Childraising? Marriage? Everyone is bewitching other people, or trying to, from the moment that a baby realizes that by crying he can bring his mother running, to the moment that he's laid in his grave to a chorus of blubbering relatives. The magic of everyday society, manipulating other people, is as commonplace an activity as eating or sleeping. Nobody learns magic. All that happens is that they start paying attention to the things that everyone else is ignoring or taking for granted: they just become aware that they are capable of performing magical acts (usually due to a teacher's or spirits' aegis).

It is in fact quite possible to manipulate the emotions of other people at a distance. Moreover, everybody's doing this to everybody else all the time. The secret of true magic, as opposed to the magic of everyday society, is not to force oneself into other people's space. Other people are given 100% free choice at all times.

Even black magicians follow this rule. They don't jump into their victim's space but rather lure people who are on a self-destructive trip to them. What makes the magic of everyday society so appallingly inept is the common use of brute force – fear, guilt, criticism, disapproval – to bend other people to your will. This is inelegant and engenders too much friction and resistance. It wastes energy (which demons eat). Everybody's just clawing at everyone else and not getting very much accomplished. It's just not an effective way of manipulating people.

Expressing anger openly at other people is an idiotic stand. To vent anger at your subordinates just guarantees that they will, in the future, conceal from you important information that you need to know. Parents forbidding their children to do something merely results in the kids hiding that activity from their parents. To express anger at people who prepare your food – for example, in a restaurant – is utterly insane.

Even with people whom you dislike or distrust, it is better to act as if you need their advice on how to proceed. This often garners valuable information and help. I was once in the situation of being in an airport, my flight cancelled, with a mob of screaming, angry passengers attacking the airline employees. I took one employee aside and remarked sympathetically how difficult it must be to work for the airline and have to take the passengers' flack. Don't you think that guy got me onto the next plane ahead of the VIP's?

Think about the times in your life when you were under someone's thumb and they really had you fuming. They actually had you bewitched. By being angry at them, by reacting, you allowed them to suck your energy. The way people impose themselves on you – jump into your space – is by making their feelings more important to you than your own feelings. They make you think constantly about them. Thus the way that you can resist bewitchment is by summarily refusing to think any thoughts whatsoever about the people who are trying to impose themselves on you. You try to ignore them completely.

Unless there is conscious expression of a feeling, a thought form expressing it, then it just builds and builds. This is how magicians bewitch for love. They build and build a feeling of love, lust, or desire for the person they are bewitching. They purposely don't express it consciously. Note that this is exactly the opposite of the way the dating game works: buying flowers and candy, sprucing up in front of the mirror, trying to impress someone, and so forth. Magicians don't do anything overt. By not expressing the feeling they lay a heavy emotional charge on the person they are bewitching until the Spirit makes the link which expresses it consciously.

What is Magic?

What magicians do is no different from what most people do. People are bewitching each other all the time, but they call it "falling in love" instead of "mutual bewitchment." They don't understand the process by which they made that emotional contact with each other across society's barriers of distrust.

According to the magical view of life, everyone is actually, beneath the surface, out to devour everyone else: to steal their power. This is the basic energy dynamic underlying the parent-child relationship. Kids steal their parents' power when they are born. This is why people with kids are more effete than childless people. Childraising is parents' futile attempt to recapture that power by dominating their kids and breaking their wills ("training" them).

Any thoughtful person who has been married for a while intuits that this is true: that there is something else, some underlying battle for power, going on beneath the surface problems in marriage which is not being acknowledged consciously. Because our society regards such doings as evil, it covers up all the manipulations that are actually going on surreptitiously with hypocrisy.

This is all right. There's nothing wrong with any of this. It's nothing to hide or be ashamed of. This is just the way nature is. Man's inhumanity to man is no worse than dogs' incaninity to dogs or cats' infelinity to cats. Humans' cruelty is just more elaborate, just as everything that humans do is more elaborate than what animals do. The animal kingdom is no buddy-buddy place, even within species. There's always a lot of competition, jealousy, and gratuitous nastiness going on. Therefore, if we want to trace out the roots of evil, we have to look beyond our own species since humans are not uniquely uptight and nasty.

On the other hand, plants are not evil at all. They harbor no evil intentions whatsoever. Even most poisonous plants have curative properties in small doses, and all plants have some sort of healing powers. Therefore, in trying to get at the problem of evil, we are dealing with a quality which is proper to animals, but not plants. The dog-eat-dog bit is universal among all beings who are able to move around, so how can it be characterized as evil? The One who invented the rule that in order to survive we must destroy other beings is responsible for this. Is God evil then?

Is magic evil? A similar question is: is sex evil? You'll notice that for the most part the people who believe that sex is evil are the same ones who believe that magic is evil. Just as up until recently our society made us feel ashamed of our normal sexual desires, so too does it make us feel afraid of our normal magical powers.

Magic is as much a part of our everyday lives as our sexual feelings are. Everybody's using magic all the time, even if they don't realize they're doing it. Of course, most people are doing it unconsciously and incompetently.

Earlier generations in our society couldn't see all the sexuality that was really going on because they were taught to be ashamed or afraid of it. So too are we taught to be afraid of or disbelieve in magic. Thus we can't see magic happening even when it's going on right before our eyes.

Seeing magic at work isn't so much a matter of discovering hidden secrets of the universe as it is a matter of changing your point of view and looking at everyday life as it is, without all the sham and hypocrisy. Just as there are all sorts of hidden sexual agendas going on between people, though less hidden now than in previous generations, so too there are lots of hidden magical agendas going on. Seeing them is just a matter of opening your eyes.

Nobody has to learn sexuality. You were already a sexual being ever since infancy. All you have to do to take command of your sexuality is to throw off your early conditioning, and go out there and *do it*. Similarly, you don't have to learn magic, because you're already doing magic all the time. All you have to do is to become conscious of what you're already doing unconsciously and unskillfully. In fact, if you're reading this sentence, you're using magic to do it. Magic is what enables you to assemble your attention. Magic is the act of holding attention fixed on a specific object, to make sense out of what is being experienced and ultimately to direct that experience.

What is Magic?

Our society is presently at the point vis a vis magic that it was at vis a vis sex a century ago. At that time sex was considered shameful. It was not spoken of openly. Then Sigmund Freud came along, and very courageously and audaciously proclaimed that it's all sex. This is something that the Hindus had been saying all along, but which was shocking to the late Victorian mentality which Freud confronted. Freud made sex intellectually respectable. This paved the way by the 1960's for the man and woman in the street to address their own sexual feelings without all the hypocrisy and pretense which characterized Victorian sexuality.

Freud didn't invent sex. All he did was point out that everyone is sexual, but they are hiding their true feelings about it. People just comply with what is expected of them in order to be considered "normal". At the present time, Carlos Castaneda and others are doing for magic what Freud did for sex a century ago. Castaneda pointed out that everyone is fundamentally doing magic all the time, albeit unconsciously and ineptly – they are just pretending they aren't doing it. Just as it took our society a good 50 years to catch up to Freud, so too will it take a good part of this present century until society's center of gravity catches up to Castaneda. But truth has a way of coming out in the end.

Magicians are not concerned with questions of good and evil. "Evil" is just a term people use to describe what they are afraid of facing within themselves, which those guys over there (the "evil" ones) are acting out openly. What you consider to be "evil" is just what you yourself are repressing; which lets you plump up your glory by feeling superior to those "evil" ones over there.

Although magicians are fundamentally anti-social, they are not unsocial. They're as outgoing and friendly as anyone else. Magicians just don't have any political agenda. They have no interest whatever in changing society. They turn their backs on it in order to change themselves. Society is inescapable. It is a magician's triumph of will to blend in without becoming dependent on society and its lies.

However, the earth herself, our mother, does have an agenda. Magicians have to be aware of and further the earth's agenda if you plan to continue living and reincarnating upon her. That agenda is pretty obvious and doesn't need to be restated here. Nonetheless the vast majority of people still keep supporting politicians and corporations which are out to destroy the earth we live on. They vote with their purchases and everyday choices to support a rampantly destructive capitalism and war economy which will – if it proceeds unchecked – end with the annihilation of the human race. Everyone can see this happening, there's nothing secret going on, but no one seems to care. Government, the media, the churches, and materialistic science are just babbling inanities while everything is burning down.

   The earth is crying. Can you hear it? Hearing the earth's sorrow is the first step in opening your heart, becoming a magician. To magicians there isn't any such thing as good or evil, just skillfulness or stupidity. It's time now for each of us as individuals to make the irrevocable choice between them. The earth and the human race *can* be saved. The earth and the human race *will* be saved. It's up to *you*.

XVII – Dreaming and Stalking

There are two kinds of magicians: dreamers and stalkers. Everyone is born either the one kind or the other. Each type has its own distinctive talents and shortcomings. However the training of the two types of magicians is quite different. To paraphrase Carlos Castaneda, dreamers shift levels of awareness in order to rearrange their everyday priorities, whereas stalkers rearrange their everyday priorities in order to shift levels of awareness (in Castaneda's nomenclature, dreamers move their assemblage points in order to lose importance; whereas stalkers lose importance in order to move their assemblage points).

One can tell dreamers from stalkers in everyday life because dreamers tend to be fearful people, whereas stalkers tend to be angry people. Fearful people are fearful precisely because they shift levels of awareness so easily that they fear going crazy. Angry people are angry at themselves because they find it so difficult to stop clinging to their everyday awareness and just let go.

Dreamers are a bit other-worldly or spaced-out. They are moody and morbid. Stalkers, by contrast, are cocky, bouncy, and intense. Married couples usually consist of a dreamer and a stalker. The dreamer is the quieter one of the two, who stays in the background. The stalker is the more outgoing and forceful one, or at least is the one who relates with other people.

Dreaming

The first goal of the practice of magic is the volitional control of one's moment-to-moment attention. When awake this is termed "stalking", and when asleep it's termed "lucid dreaming". Here we use the term "lucid dreaming" to mean what Castaneda referred to as *dreaming*. Lucid dreaming is dreaming in which you know that you are asleep and are dreaming. If you have never had this experience, what normally occurs is that you're dreaming along as usual, and then suddenly you "wake up" and realize that you are dreaming. At that point you are able to rationalize as you can when you are awake, but within the context of the world of dreams. For example, if you want to fly, you can take off and fly. Lucid dreaming differs from normal dreaming in that you have more volitional control over what will happen, as you do in waking life; but you are using the rules of dreaming.

I've used lucid dreaming to do experiments. Once I wanted to check whether my senses of smell and taste were as operative in dreaming as sight and hearing are. I waited until I had a lucid dream, and then I smelled and ate something. Thus I learned that these senses work in the dream state also.

On another occasion I was lucidly dreaming that I had a wine glass in my hand, and I wanted to see if I smashed it on the ground, whether it would smash just as it does in waking (it did). There are some good books on lucid dreaming presently available.[1] Lucid dreaming is a gateway to astral projection.

Normal dreams are unimportant insofar as their content is concerned. Nonetheless they should be recollected and written down to make dreaming an important activity. This will bestow upon dreaming the same attention and care that you bring to bear upon your waking activities. There's no point in wasting time interpreting dreams unless they're quite disturbing, or contain obvious messages. Lucid dreams, on the other hand you must pay strict attention to. You must not try to control them, at first anyway. Just watch everything that happens. Write it all down afterwards.

To lucidly dream, or even to remember normal dreams, requires a lot of energy. You have to minimize self-importance, and not engage in orgasmic sex very often. This means once a month at most; at best, never. Dreams are easier to remember if you put a cap or bandana on when you go to sleep. Lucid dreaming is also easier if your wear a "dream cap" when you sleep. Once you are in a lucid dream, call upon your spirit guides to come forward, and they will (in one fashion or another) make their appearance and show you what to do.

What both dreamers and stalkers are striving to accomplish is to make the line between being awake and being asleep thinner. This blends the two states. It makes waking more dream-like, and it imposes rational order on dreaming.

In everyday life the wall between being awake and being asleep is thinnest when you suddenly hit upon the right solution to a problem. For example: "Do I have enough money? (swift mental calculation) ... I do!" That sudden realization of knowing something directly, that click, is a state of mind midway between waking and dreaming.

Dreamers work on erasing that curtain to make it easier to go back and forth between the two states. You do this by dropping off to sleep immediately, and then waking up refreshed and ready for action. You should be in a very good mood to go to sleep. You should look forward to sleeping as an adventure, not as a drug to blot out your consciousness. You must approach going to sleep with élan.

It helps to concentrate on sounds in order to drop off to sleep. The trick to falling asleep on demand is to allow dream images to flood into your mind in a jumble. Let these hypnagogic images of your mind's eye flow by rather than grabbing onto them.

When you awaken in the morning you should immediately splash some water on your face to wake yourself up. No lolling in bed for magicians! To shake off a feeling of sleepiness upon awakening or during the day, it helps to sit or roll on the ground. This picks up the earth's refreshing energy.

Gazing is an exercise which helps to efface the barrier between dreaming and waking. It can also provide a doorway to astral projection, by entering directly into the gazing scene. Developing your psychic vision (and your other psychic abilities) is really just a matter of paying attention to the little things going on around you. Most people miss out on the magic of life because they have all their attention focused on the hurly-burly hustle-bustle. To develop your psychic vision you have to slow down a bit and pay attention to the little, peripheral details rather than the big-screen image; and also not focus directly on things, but rather look out of the corner of your eye at them (as it were). All gazing exercises begin by relaxing your gaze by lightly crossing your eyes, in order to create a double image.

This is in fact what your two eyes are seeing all the time – two images. This is how newborns see the world. It was your social training (in your first few months of life) which taught you how to "blend" these two images into one scene. The effort involved in maintaining this moment-to-moment focus on one image is actually quite a strain; but you (like all adults) have become so accustomed to the effort involved that you don't realize how unnatural and uncomfortable it is, and how much visual information you lose in the process. By relaxing your gaze and returning your attention to the actual scene (double image) which is presenting itself to your field of vision, your eyes are freed up to grasp subtle nuances lost in single-image vision.

For introductory instructions, see the "Photograph Gazing" chapter of my book *Magical Living*. To gaze, cross your eyes lightly and look at things which are close to you, not far away. Look at little things very closely: scrutinize small things on the ground, or the bark of a tree up close. You shouldn't cross your eyes too tightly. It has to be a really loose and relaxed lack of focus. It's not a fuzziness, but a double image, and relaxed. In gazing the feeling is more important than the vision.

Don't stare at the thing you're looking at. Glance at it and away and back again; or just to the side of it, as you do to see things at night. You don't look directly at things unless they are very solid-looking and are trying to show you something; that is to say, if they are trying to capture your attention.

Try this: align two objects – one in front of the other (one foreground, one background, but not in a direct line – i.e. a space in between). Gaze at them giving each one equal importance. This balancing is difficult to accomplish at first because the initial tendency is to wobble back and forth. Once you've got the balance, stare in the middle. As you're staring in the middle, keep the two objects in balance. You aren't looking at them, although they are in your field of vision. Another good exercise is to watch the steam in the morning as it comes off the earth; this is how the earth sends you her

What is Magic?

messages. Soak up the knowledge of the steam from the earth; *feel* it.

At first it's difficult to see people's auras because your eyes are unaccustomed to seeing people as anything other than objects of your desire. That is to say, they come on to you as solid objects to which you feel you must respond. In order to see anyone's aura, especially people close to you, you must first hold your breath and watch.

Watch first around the tummy, as here is where the fibers of light originate from. It is best if you hold your stomach to prevent your own fibers from reaching out and intermingling with your subject's. In other words, rather than looking at a person's eyes and smile (which is what your desire nature seeks), you should take in one whole breath and keep it there while you search out your subject. At first you will "see" some fine color differences or emphases of light. You will also feel a little tightness in the pit of your stomach.

There are different ways of perceiving auras. Another way to do it is to shift your weight and your eyes around the person's umbilicus. Also, you might try looking when people have just eaten, as it is easier in most cases to see auras after a meal. Again, always look at the stomach region. The trick is to let the people feel at ease with you, thus letting their light fibers stretch out towards you so they are more visible than protected, scared, contracted light fibers are.

The basic training of dreamers is in astral projection. There are basically two doorways into astral projection. One of them begins in lucid dreaming. The other, which is for very talented dreamers, starts from the position of being awake. This means by gazing and entering into the gazing scene. Since I can't do astral projection (I'm a stalker, and even my gazing is rather clunky compared to that of my dreamer friends and students), I can't describe this from personal experience. For more information on this subject see Robert Monroe's book *Journeys Out of the Body*.[2]

Stalking

Where dreaming involves volitional control of the dream state, stalking involves volitional control of the waking state. In particular, this refers to conscious control of your behavior and relations with other people.

Stalking can be defined as a means for winning all the wars by losing all the battles. Stalking is a technique for threading your way around people and disentangling yourself from other people's webs. This means being imperturbable and slippery, and not drawing undue attention to yourself.

Stalking is patient and kind; stalking is not jealous or boastful; it is not arrogant or rude. Stalking does not insist on its own way; it is not irritable or resentful; it does not rejoice at wrong, but rejoices in the right. Stalking bears all things, hopes all things, endures all things. Up to a point, anyway.

In order to fit into society, you have to lie to other people all day long every day. You have to pretend to be somebody you're not. Inside, you (like everyone else) feel wracked by doubts and fears and self-hatred; but in order get by in the outside world you have to project a false front of self-assurance, and not discuss openly what you're really feeling inside.

People just don't want the truth, so you have to give them what they want. Magicians, like everyone else, have to constantly tell lies to other people in order to get by. However, magicians, unlike average people, consider it unskillful to lie to themselves.

To be a magician means to know what you want in your heart, not your mind. This is not what other people and society say you should want. If your heart is closed, as most people's hearts are, then you have to get this information via deduction, by active imagination, or by channeling it from spirit advisors.

In any case magicians don't lie to themselves. They look at themselves squarely in the mirror and accept whatever they find there. This means good stuff, bad stuff, forbidden sexual desires, feelings they shouldn't be feeling, stupid things

What is Magic?

they've done that they're ashamed of, whatever. It's all the same. It's just a bunch of actors on a stage.

Stalking, which entails being nice to other people, is not necessarily faking it. Black magicians and psychopaths do fake being nice in order to get their way with people. To a white magician, being nice means being genuinely open, receptive, gentle, and inviting. It means treating other people civilly, politely, and respectfully. It means just letting them go their own way and do their thing (as long as it's not in your space). Magicians don't project their own self-importance and self-pity onto others. This doesn't mean being a wuss – not at all. Stalking entails coming down firmly and ruthlessly the first second there's any kind of bad faith or invasion of space going on.

The trick to stalking is to be able to see the other person's point of view objectively, whether you agree with it or not. Since scarcely anyone in our society is capable of doing this, stalkers have a tremendous advantage over average people. Stalking requires indifference; which isn't so much a listlessness per se, as it is a disinclination to become involved if you can possibly avoid it. And, because you are personally uninvolved, you can see all the ego games which everyone around you is playing with crystal clarity: to finesse other people, you have to be able to see clearly what you are finessing against. Then, when you do have to act, then you act with a cold, hard, ruthlessness. Both white and black magic use the same techniques. Whether these are employed because you genuinely have no importance of your own to project; or whether it's done to disarm people and win their trust in order to destroy them; makes no difference. Stalking is stalking.

The art of stalking is characterized by four virtues. Although different thinkers on the subject describe these qualities in very different ways, it is obvious that they are talking about the same thing: the main objective of stalking is stalking yourself. This is the opposite of fooling yourself (what society has taught you to do).

Castaneda describes the four moods of the stalker as being *patient, sweet, ruthless and cunning*.[3] Chögyam Trungpa describes the warrior's path which consists of the four dignities *meek, perky, outrageous and inscrutable*.[4] What's being described in either case is a set of techniques for getting by, through, and around other people instead of banging into them. When you bang into people, you lose energy. Stalking is a strategy for disentangling yourself from the webs of light fibers in which you are ensnared by, and in turn ensnare, the people around you. It's a means for erasing your lower self by detaching from taking things personally, by taking things in stride instead.

Part of stalker training is to deliberately put yourself in highly unfamiliar, disorienting, even uncomfortable situations; and to adjust to them with complete élan. Doing this quite naturally detaches you from your customary moods and concerns. This deliberate masquerading can actually be quite an enjoyable exercise. This is why people find travel to foreign countries so pleasurable and liberating. The purpose of stalking is to shake you out of your routines and petty obsessions. You stop clinging to the things which are familiar and important. As you dissolve your customary moods and concerns, you lighten up and enjoy yourself once more.

Stalking is furtive and devious, but that's only because people are full of crap. If everyone was a stalker, there would be no need to stalk. You could just go to people openly and honestly, and ask them whatever you wanted of them. You could trust people. However, the society we live in forbids openness and honesty, and it rewards trust with betrayal. Magicians have to be consummate phonies because everyone around them is phony. Magicians, however, have no interest in showing off or making an impression on others.

The goal of stalker training is learning to become invisible (in the Ralph Ellison sense, rather than the H.G. Wells sense). Becoming invisible doesn't mean that you become transparent, but rather that you become *unnoticeable*. You learn how to unhook yourself from other people altogether: to make other people completely unimportant to you; and thereby you become completely unimportant to them. This means seeking no validation or mirroring from other people (and they in turn will seek none from you).

What is Magic?

From other people's point of view, you seem like whatever thought forms they want to put on you (rather like everyone did to Peter Sellers in *Being There*); but there are no undercurrents going on. It's not like they can't see you; it's like they don't notice you, because there's no one there to notice. Even when you speak to people and look them in the eye, they won't have a clear "memory" of having interacted with you; any more than they notice a pebble on the road (unless you've connected with them on a light fiber level, e.g. by smiling at them).

A beggar, lunatic, or black magician does this to play upon people's shame, to induce fear so that people won't relate to them. However, this is still to be hooked up to other people. The way it should be done is by being completely cold and detached. This is beyond the Place of No Pity: you no longer pity anyone or ask for pity yourself, so you don't really have much energy (expectation) going back and forth between yourself and other people.

This is why it is important to open your heart first, otherwise you will be cold and detached always, which is also an imbalance. The point is that you switch it off and on as prompted by the Spirit. When the Spirit prompts you to pour out great love (on or with another person), you do it – you do exchange light fiber energy. But unless specifically prompted by the Spirit (by your true feelings), you clam up on a light fiber level. You don't react to anything which anyone lays on you, whether good or bad, nor do you seek anything from anyone. You truly don't give a damn one way or the other (this doesn't mean you get lazy: you stay ready to move at once at the slightest sign from the Spirit).

This is on a light fiber level; on a thought form level you go through all the motions, dot all the i's and cross all the t's. But you are unhooked from it, and from other people. You don't care in the least whether other people respond to you or not, or reflect you, or anything of the sort. You just don't care.

The only way to unhook yourself from other people is to open your heart to them. Yogananda said that if you can open your heart to just one person, you can open your heart to everyone. It could also have been expressed as: "If you can unhook yourself from just one person, you can unhook yourself from everyone."

When you are unhooked from everyone, they can't bother you anymore, no matter what they do or don't do. The easiest way to arrive at this conviction of the heart is by being rejected and rejected and rejected by other people, until all your expectations of them have bitten the dust.

This is the white magician's way of unhooking yourself from people. Black magicians completely close their hearts to everyone (act shamelessly). By opening your heart to people you can hook or unhook at will, as prompted by the Spirit through omens and signs, rather than being hooked up to them all the time, and to be dragged up and down by other people's moods and whims.

What you are unhooking here are the importance coverings on your light fibers (as explained in the "Black Magicians" chapter of my book *Thought Forms*). When you unhook yours, they automatically disengage from everyone else's.

Where the basic training of dreamers is astral projection (approached either through the cultivation of lucid dreaming or by gazing and entering into the gazing scene), the basic training of stalkers is recapitulation. This is a technique for reliving memories of your past. It is far more vivid and emotionally compelling than ordinary remembering. It's more like dreaming, although you are definitely awake.

When you recapitulate a memory you are actually back there in the scene again. This time around, however, you are more detached. It's as if you are both in it and watching it from a distance at the same time. You can feel not only what you felt then, but also the feelings of everyone else in the scene.

The technique of recapitulation is very simple, and in various guises has long been well-known in certain schools of psychiatry.[5] A complete explanation of the theory and practice of recapitulation appears in my book *The Great Wheel*). In recapitulation (as opposed to running past life regressions) you don't merely watch the scene unfold passively, as you do when running past lives. In addition, you

What is Magic?

pull your feelings (light fibers) back out of the scene you are watching by sucking them back into your navel with a sharp, indrawn breath.

How can you escape from the bondage you are in? This can only be done by shifting your viewpoint until you truly understand that:

1) You brought these circumstances upon yourself. You have no one to blame but yourself for the situation you are in.

2) It isn't really bondage at all but rather the path to liberation. That's why you brought this on yourself in the first place – to learn that lesson.

How do you make this shift in your viewpoint? How can you come to clearly see how you did this to yourself? This is done by recapitulating the memories of those decisions – the decisions that brought you here. And once you've seen them clearly by reliving them, you can then change those decisions if you want to by sucking them (the light fibers attached to them) back into your navel with an indrawn breath.

Recapitulation is a purgative and liberating technique. Reliving those memories of the decisive moments in your life, particularly the traumatic and joyous ones, just loosens you up and makes you feel younger. Recapitulation is actually a doorway, like astral projection is a doorway. Advanced stalkers such as Castaneda could recapitulate memories of lives of people they'd never even met.[6]

It's good for natural-born dreamers to learn stalking techniques, and it's good for natural-born stalkers to learn dreaming techniques. The goal in either case is to expand your awareness and open up you to what's really going on: to unfold your wings and fly into the unknown.

Notes:

[1] LaBerge, Stephen, *Lucid Dreaming*, Ballantine NYC 1986; LaBerge, Stephen and Rheingold, Howard, *Exploring the World of Lucid Dreaming*, Ballantine NYC 1990.

[2] Monroe, Robert, *Journeys Out of the Body*, Anchor NYC 1971. See also the Monroe Institute website www.monroeinstitute.org. Another good book is Ophiel (Clarence Peach), *The Art and Practice of Astral Projection*, Weiser NYC 1961.

[3] Castaneda, Carlos, *The Power of Silence*, Simon & Schuster NYC 1987.

[4] Trungpa, Chőgyam, *Shambhala*, Bantam NYC 1986.

[5] see e.g. Penfield, Wilder, *Memory Mechanisms*, *AMA Archives of Neurology and Psychiatry 67*, 1952.

[6] Castaneda, Carlos, *The Wheel of Time*, Washington Square Press NYC 1998.

XVIII – Magic and Sex

Becoming a magician involves taking a good, hard look at yourself and the society of which you are a part. Magicians are supreme realists who must look at how things actually are, not how they would prefer them to be or how society pretends that they are. In particular, this means taking a straight look at your sexuality. It means seeing clearly what you're really feeling inside, as opposed to your images of how you think you're supposed to feel. Along with fear of death, sexual repression is society's chief means of enslaving you.

The fact is, human beings are not biologically hard-wired for nuclear families within a framework of heterosexual, monogamous marriage. This is a recent (Neolithic) accretion. Amongst many present-day hunting / gathering tribes, such as the Amazonian Yanomamis for example, there's a great deal of what we would term sexual promiscuity going on. Everyone sleeps with everyone else, and infant care is shared by all the adults in the social group. This is part of a general picture in which there is little sense of personal property: anthropologists studying such tribes frequently have a hard time hanging onto their cameras and tape recorders. As a consequence, there is much less sexual possessiveness and jealousy in hunting / gathering societies than in our society. The point is that monogamous marriage – and the sexual jealousy which sustains it – is not necessarily an innate trait of humans as it is for certain other animal species.

It is similar with heterosexuality. There have been human societies, such as ancient Greece, where homosexuality was practiced as openly as heterosexuality. And except for people in certain very repressed societies in which extramarital sex was unthinkable (such as the Aztecs, who punished adultery with death and really meant it), anyone who's ever been married for a while knows that the temptation to adultery, if not the actual deed, is ever-present. Does anyone really believe than human males are naturally monogamous? Or females, for that matter?

The agricultural base of our society began to crumble two hundred years ago with the advent of the industrial revolution. Its final dissolution has come in the last half-century. As the agricultural base of society fell apart, so too did the social structures, such as nuclear families and monogamous marriage, which supported it.

This is not necessarily a bad thing. Society itself isn't necessarily dissolving: it's evolving. Calls for a return to traditional family values aren't going to work unless there is a concomitant return to family-style agriculture as a viable lifestyle for most of the population. This is unlikely to happen.

Moreover, traditional family values were a sham even when they were commonplace. There were no more happy marriages back then than there are now. All there were, were unhappy couples who kept their mouths shut because they had no choice. The linchpin which held monogamous marriage in place for so long was the impossibility of divorce, either because it was out-and-out illegal, or because of fear of what the neighbors might say. Monogamous marriage was the norm to which one had to conform. This doesn't mean that it serves the emotional and biological needs of human beings – it doesn't. Like warfare, monogamous marriage serves society's needs, but not the needs of individual people.

The soaring divorce rate in our society is not something to be alarmed about. Rather, it is an indication that our concept of marriage is in need of an overhaul. The "live happily forever" image of monogamous marriage is just that – an image. The legalization of homosexual marriage is a tremendous step forward in the right direction.

What is "normal" sexuality in our society anyway? Underneath the superficial niceties, it is normal that men regard women as prey. Women are seen as trophies to be conquered. The bulk of most men's thoughts revolve around fantasies of sexual conquest of the women they know, or see on the street, or on television, or the internet. Men's talk amongst themselves about women when there are no women present is far coarser and more degrading than women imagine. Most pornography, which represents the average

What is Magic?

male's fantasy world, is shamelessly gross and bristles with hatred of women.

As a result, it is "normal" in our society that women have to be on their guard every single second that they are around men. They are taught to fear that, if they are given the slightest opportunity to do so, men will attack them by jumping into their space in one way or another. And, of course, men have to be constantly hiding their real thoughts and intentions. The war between the sexes is one way in which our society keeps people isolated from each other, and in a constant state of anxious striving.

Society uses sex to teach people to be phony and to hate themselves. Women are taught to hate their looks and their bodies. Men are taught to hate their gentle, tender feelings as opening the door to homosexuality. People just can't relax and enjoy sex. They either make it their chief source of shame or their chief source of glory. Men are driven by sex and women are on the defensive against it. Instead of encouraging us to accept ourselves and our sexuality, our society trains us to be ashamed of ourselves and to hide our natural feelings from other people and from ourselves, or to twist them into something ugly. Thus, "normal" sexuality in our society is a rather nasty and loveless predator and prey setup.

Sex is not innately ugly. What makes it ugly is our society's belief that it is ugly. People acting on that belief make it into something ugly. Freud pointed all this out a century ago, but our society still hasn't got the point yet, although it's more enlightened about sex now than it was in Freud's day.

Not all societies are so predatory and inhibited about sex as ours is. The setup now is purposely designed to encourage people involved in intimate relationships to lie to one another; and to force people to lie to themselves. The core of your social conditioning, as Freud noted, is based upon teaching you to fear your own natural sexual desires. Your sense of shame is like a bull's nose ring which your society uses to herd you about. You were taught from infancy to feel ashamed of quite natural feelings and impulses (such as homosexual desire, which pretty much everyone feels at one time or another); and at the same time you were taught to glory in your shamelessness (your closed-hearted sense of superiority to other people). In other words, the very things that you *should* feel ashamed of – that in your heart of hearts you *are* ashamed of – namely your phony, self-important posturing and your supercilious feelings of superiority to other people – you were taught to feel proud of; and your perfectly natural sexual desires shame you. Sexual repression is the root of all emotional repression – i.e. self-hatred. This sexual shame (along with fear of death) is how society enslaves you.

Where does all the bully-boy violence and rage in American society come from – the shoot-em-up movies and video games; the obsession with guns and the glory in warfare; the shameless hatred of black people and Native Americans; the incessant wars against helpless little countries which are no threat to America, and from which there is nothing to gain? Babies are not aficionados of pathological violence; therefore it must be our social conditioning which makes us angry Angry ANGRY! It is our society which gains from our individual rage and frustration (which is the result of our denial of our true feelings). It's people furiously denying their own sexual desires which makes them so aggressive and full of senseless rage; and society channels that rage into conspicuous consumption and "patriotism". If everyone felt whole and content and happy in their hearts it would be bad for the economy. And where would they find cannon fodder for their endless, futile wars?

Earlier generations in our society were even taught to feel ashamed of masturbating (as if 99% of the population doesn't masturbate)! That sort of Victorian hypocrisy seems amusing to us now. But remember that in the 2004 U.S. presidential election homosexual marriage was a major campaign issue (to divert popular attention away from that country's substantive problems). Indeed, it wasn't until the 2004 election that it became obvious how large a proportion of the American electorate – not to mention the President himself – are repressed homosexuals. Else why would they give a damn what other people do or don't do?

What is Magic?

Instead of teaching you to hate yourself by denying your normal sexual desires, society could have accomplished much the same thing by making you fear your normal hunger (instead of your sexuality) – i.e., get everyone to pretend that they are never hungry, and to hate themselves for secretly eating. In that scenario, in order to eat you would have to slink to the seamy side of town, where the grocery stores were located, under cover of nightfall; make your selection and purchase it with averted eyes; then quickly retire to an abandoned building or under a bridge to feed.

On the other hand, everybody would be running around naked and screwing openly on the street corners. Women's magazines would be filled with the latest kinky perversions rather than recipes; and men's magazines would feature provocative photos of beefsteak and lobster. Thanksgiving and Christmas would be celebrated with wild sex orgies instead of feasts. But anorexia would be the norm, and fat people would be viewed as they were during the siege of Leningrad. Burping and farting would be the supreme *faux pas*. The ultimate benefit to society would be much the same as it is now – everyone would be ashamed of themselves; hate themselves for being so naughty and not fulfilling society's arbitrary and impossible expectations; lie to themselves and their intimate associates about their true desires; and everyday life and relationships would be a complete sham, just like they are now. Society would have everyone miserable and jumping through hoops on command, just like it does now.

Fifty years ago the very thought of oral sex disgusted most people; now the very thought turns most people on. Similarly at the present time the very thought of homosexuality disgusts most people, and for the same reason that oral sex used to: because people are actually turned on by it and have to repress that desire by substituting its opposite (shame). Disgust is how you pretend to yourself that you would not enjoy doing the very same thing which disgusts you. Else why would you care?

It is the fact that our society is so sexually repressed that makes men so predatory and women so defensive. If people were open about sex to begin with instead of pretending they aren't feeling what they're feeling – forcing themselves to squelch their true feelings – there wouldn't be all this weirdness and power games connected to sexuality going on. Rather, sex would be as matter-of-fact and taken for granted as eating and sleeping are. Sex would be no big deal, just as it's no big deal in hunting / gathering societies. As an example, take Tahiti when Cook and Bligh got there.

It's people squelching down on their natural sexual desires that makes sex such an obsession, taking such perverted and ugly forms. As Freud pointed out, sexual repression is the reason why most people are so neurotic, unhappy, and out-of-kilter with one another and themselves.

=> Why do you suppose people don't look one another directly in the eye when addressing each other except for the few seconds required for politeness? Looking people in the eye is considered invasive because it is sexual.

Society has taught you to pretend that you don't feel sexual attraction to the people you meet. This is not to say that you should turn every encounter with another person into a staring match. Quite the contrary, that's very inept. To outstare other people is to invade their space, precisely because it *is* so sexual. Lunatics and drunks sometimes do this to tease normal people by provoking their shame (making them avert their eyes); but magicians never do this since it blows their cover.

=> Why do you suppose your basic stance with strangers is one of distrust rather than trust? Why can't you just relax with strangers, not to mention your friends and acquaintances?

This is because you fear that if you let down your constant guard they will come on to you sexually. You have been trained to fear that making yourself vulnerable to people is inviting them to attack you. That is why, in spite of how much time you spend talking with other people, you hardly ever say anything to them, or they to you. When was the last time you spoke of what you're really feeling inside to *anybody*?

=> Why do you consider certain thoughts to be unthinkable, such as feeling sexually turned on by a member

What is Magic?

of the same sex; by your own child or siblings; by a neighbor's child; by thy neighbor's wife? Society says that such thoughts are bad, and should be repressed immediately.

You are taught to reject these thoughts even before they are formulated as conscious thoughts. This is why most people fail to recognize such impulses within themselves: not because they don't have them, but because they immediately stomp on them before the thoughts can reach conscious awareness. This a lie most people in our society tell themselves about their own sexual desires.

Suppose that having such thoughts is indeed bad. Then the thing to do is to just acknowledge the thought and then drop it: "Yes, this thought which popped up is not such a good thought, so let's stop thinking it."

This is not difficult to do. You already do this with lots of thoughts, such as angry thoughts. It's called processing. You are not compelled to act out every single whim and fancy that darts into your mind. However, that is not how most people deal with so-called improper sexual thoughts. Because of their social training, most people don't even let such thoughts arise; they squelch them before the thoughts become conscious (this is not really true. *All* desires are conscious, if only for a split second, before they are just as consciously repressed. You can see this take place in people's eyes: their instantaneous recognition of what's really going on, and then their lightning stomp on their own feelings as their fear takes over).

Whether feelings of sexual turn-on are bad or not, is not the point. The point is that they are *normal*. Everybody at one time or another feels sexually turned on by people and practices that society says they are not supposed to feel turned on by. These sorts of feelings stem from other lifetimes and realities. Your children, parents, siblings, friends etc. in this lifetime were your lovers in other lifetimes. The sexual feelings towards them often remain along with the love felt for them.

In an unrepressed society, people would feel these kinds of feelings and then just drop them. It wouldn't be any big deal. It only becomes a big deal – an obsession – when people are forced to clamp down hard on themselves and pretend to themselves and other people that they aren't feeling what they're really feeling inside.

Sexual repression and sexual fantasy – shame and glory – are the chief support structures which prop up your lower self. When you start examining your true sexual desires objectively is when you start to lose your lower self. This point is so very important that it bears repeating: when you can feel your normal sexual desires without any tinge of shame or glory, then you are beginning to connect to your higher self.

How can you tell if you're lying to yourself? If there is anything which someone else is doing openly which harms no one but which really bugs you, or makes you feel superior (judgmental) of them, then that's a good indication that you wish you could be doing the same thing but are repressing that feeling. If there is any sexual act which you find particularly disgusting, that likely means that you would like to do it yourself but are repressing your desire. At any rate, you see it in yourself.

For example, homophobes are homosexuals in severe denial. They are people who hate themselves because they inwardly feel feelings which they are terrified of acknowledging consciously. As a result they project that hatred outwardly onto the people who are expressing these feelings openly.

Magicians can't afford this sort of lying to themselves. They have to take a good look at everything going on inside of them, whether it's good or bad, applauded by society or condemned by it. Becoming a magician requires true self-discipline based on open acknowledgement of what you are really feeling inside, and conscious selection or rejection of which impulses will be acted upon and which not. Thus to a magician nothing is unthinkable.

In spite of how you have been trained by society, it is not true that other people are there to prop up your flagging self-esteem. That is not other people's purpose on this earth. The next time you have a glory fantasy, a daydream of sex or romance, take a minute out and look at the role you've cast the

What is Magic?

other person in. Ask yourself, if the situation were reversed, whether you'd really fawn that much over someone else?

How much of the content of your fantasies involves you appreciating the other person as opposed to rankly exploiting them? This is perhaps the central difference between ordinary daydreaming and Creative Visualization of being in a relationship. In ordinary daydreaming you are controlling everything. In Creative Visualization the other person is making all the suggestions about what will happen next. In C.V. there's a sense that you are really with the other person, not just ordering him or her about. The other person isn't just a tassel on your ego, put there for your gratification, but rather is warm and alive.

For magicians it's perfectly all right to have consensual sex with anyone you want to. This means heterosexual or homosexual, inside or outside of marriage. The only rule is that no lying is going on. Magicians don't care what society or other people might think of them. Therefore, they're not inhibited sexually, or any other way.

Magicians' discipline arises from within. They respond to the logic of the situation and their concern for other people's feelings. They are not motivated by fear of what might be thought of them or said about them. They don't have anything to hide, least of all from themselves.

Becoming a magician doesn't mean casting spells and invoking spirits. It means taking a good, hard, objective look at everything that is going on inside of you instead of hypocritically pretending that you aren't feeling what you're actually feeling inside. It means taking a good, hard objective look at the reality you create for yourself every day. *All anger is self-anger and all disgust is self-disgust.* Becoming a magician means, e.g. when you feel anger, to examine what it is you are really angry at (not the lie you are telling yourself). You are not angry at other people – what you are angry at is yourself, for allowing the other person to bend you out of shape. Similarly, becoming a magician means that when you feel disgust, to examine what it is you are *really* disgusted at. You are not disgusted with other people – you are disgusted with yourself for being such a phony; for repressing whatever it is that the other person is doing openly.

It is only when you learn to truly accept yourself – which means acknowledging what's really going on inside you on an emotional level – that you are in a position to truly love yourself. When you can accept and love yourself, then you are in a position to truly accept and love others, and to be loved by them in return.

What is Magic?

XIX – Bibliography of Magic

There is probably more malarky written about magic than any other topic on earth. Most books on the subjects of mysticism and occultism, particularly those from the nineteenth and early twentieth centuries, are mostly empty talk. Many of the pagan-wiccan books you find on the New Age shelf at bookstores are lists of the trappings of magic without any of the core. They list spells for this and spells for that, but give no information on how to make spells work.

Fortunately, just in the past forty years, some very valuable information has been published, largely from shamanic sources. The alpha and omega of modern magical theory and practice are the oeuvres of Carlos Castaneda. Castaneda was a Peruvian anthropologist who, while working on his doctoral dissertation for UCLA in 1961, stumbled upon a Yaqui Indian magician named don Juan Matus.

Don Juan took Carlos as his apprentice and introduced him to an ancient Toltec praxis which has far-reaching implications for the future of the human race. This praxis consists of training in an alternate form of cognition than that which we learn from our society.

Castaneda's work has sparked a firestorm of controversy. It has been thoroughly rejected by the academic community, which is not surprising considering the mindless bigotry and intellectual persecution which characterize present-day academia.

However, Castaneda has also split the New Age community into pro- and anti- factions. The things he says are so off-the-wall, and so alien to most people's everyday experience of the world, that unless you yourself have had similar experiences (as I have had) it's difficult to understand – much less accept – the premises of Castaneda's teachings.

Moreover, there are internal inconsistencies in the books which critics point out in the effort to discredit him, even though Castaneda himself said that part of becoming a magician is erasing your personal history and covering your tracks (this is the essence of stalking). Also the fact that

Castaneda was a womanizer is cited by his critics to deflect attention away from his message, although Castaneda himself certainly took no pains to hide that facet of his personality.

You have to decide for yourself what you will believe and take as truth. I pretty much take Castaneda at face value because everything in his books which I have been able to verify from my own experience has proven correct. My own spiritual path came out of discoveries I made while tripping on psychedelic drugs and plants. These experiences affected me profoundly and left me with lots of questions which I needed to resolve, and the only place I've found useful information on this subject is in Castaneda's books. Moreover, my one meeting with Castaneda in person did more than impress me – it utterly floored me. I know for a fact, from my own experience with him, that this man was, at the very least, a most powerful magician; whereas all I've seen amongst his detractors and critics are phonies and liars.

Wholly apart from the ooga-booga stuff, Castaneda's books contain the most cogent analysis and critique of everyday life that I've ever seen. Most of the information about the nature of the self, reality, time and space, and the body given in this book originates in Castaneda.

The corpus of Castaneda's works actually constitutes a map – an indispensable map for the spiritual traveler. This map describes the way stations (in Castaneda's nomenclature, positions of the assemblage point) along the spiritual path. These are all places – or better said, peak moments in every true spiritual seeker's life – when large parts of the lower self are shed and new facets of the higher self are revealed. At these moments the seeker permanently reaches new levels of wisdom and power.

Some of these places, such as Stopping the World and Seeing the Human Mold, are well-known and are described elsewhere in spiritual literature under different names. For example, Stopping the World is known elsewhere as *samadhi*, *satori*, or *kensho*. However other places, such as the Place of No Pity, Losing the Human Form, and Silent Knowledge, are described nowhere else except in Castaneda's books. I can aver the existence of some of these places from my own

What is Magic?

personal experience; others I am still shooting for. They are places of unhooking yourself from your societal conditioning by a superhuman letting go – a direct boost of energy from the Spirit.

If you are going on a journey, it is helpful to have a clear map devised by those who have passed that way before. Castaneda's books are the best map I have found. I trust the spiritual information they contain unreservedly. You would be well-advised to do the same.

My spirit guides use Castaneda's system as the basis for the training they have given me. They employ his concepts and nomenclature, but with their own slant on the subject and their own techniques. Castaneda's training depended heavily upon the *nagual* teacher don Juan's presence. What my spirits are trying to do is to present a heuristic system which will enable people to work on their own, under the direction of spirit guides and nature spirits rather than a *nagual* teacher.

Somebody, somewhere, some time, somehow has to stand up for the truth, no matter how unfashionable that is or how unpopular it makes the person. Castaneda was smeared and vilified for the precise same reason that Freud was (and continues to be) smeared and vilified: what he says cuts too close to the truth. Freud and Castaneda both pointed out certain vistas that society doesn't want you to see. They realized certain facts which society doesn't want you to realize.

If the human race is to survive, it had better get to work fast on finding some new intent, because the intent it's following now is the intent of self-destruction. What Castaneda has brought us is the most important new information which our civilization has received in the past several millennia. It will take the human race several centuries more to reconstruct the edifice which don Juan described to Castaneda. It's about time we stopped the endless, mindless babbling and posturing, and rolled up our sleeves and got to work; and Castaneda is the obvious place to begin.

If you're only going to read one of the Castaneda books, or if you just want to dabble, I suggest reading the third book of the 10 book series, *Journey to Ixtlan*. This book presents the most important concepts for the general spiritual seeker. Otherwise, if you are serious about becoming a magician, you should read all the books in order, starting from *The Teachings of Don Juan* through *The Active Side of Infinity*.

Additionally, Castaneda left behind an organization devoted to promulgating one aspect of don Juan's teachings which he calls Tensegrity. This is a set of physical exercises used to conserve and enhance your personal energy. I would describe them as similar to Tai Chi but more intense and angular. He wrote a book on this subject, *Magical Passes*, and sponsored some videos which illustrate how these exercises should be carried out, and left an organization to promote them.

Besides Castaneda's work, some of don Juan's other apprentices have also left accounts of their training. The best of these is *The Witch's Dream* by Florinda Donner, which is a description of a different praxis than that taught by don Juan. It gives a different point of view on the core issue of what magic is all about, namely turning the wheel of chance – i.e. making one's own luck. This is expressed in the life stories of numerous people whom Donner met in her training by a Venezuelan witch. Donner's later book *Being-In-Dreaming* is not quite as good, nor is Taisha Abelar's account of her training by don Juan, *The Sorcerer's Crossing*. However both books are valuable in presenting different parts of don Juan's praxis from other points of view, particularly from the female perspective. Armando Torres' *Encounters with the Nagual* is a collection of transcribed Castaneda lectures and informal talks which is also an invaluable resource.

My own books, *Magical Living*, *Thought Forms*, and *The Great Wheel* were written, as noted above, to show average people who live in a workaday world how to understand and spiritualize their lives – to step into the world of magic – without radically altering their lifestyles. I've been at pains to try to explain how the world of magic takes off from the world of everyday life, how one shades into the other, by using simple techniques that don't require much discipline (since I have so little myself).

What is Magic?

Magical Living is for beginners. It presents a smorgasbord of techniques and inspirational essays which are aimed at presenting the core concepts of magic in everyday terms. *Thought Forms* is for advanced students. It has a lot of psychological explanations, and it presents a formal course of magical training (the course of my own training as directed by my spirit guides) based on shamanistic and Jungian techniques.

Thought Forms is also the first book in the projected Astrology of Consciousness trilogy, in which the astrological symbolism of the personal planets sun, Mercury, moon, and Venus is used to model consciousness. *Thought Forms* discusses the operation of everyday mind in terms of the astrological symbolism of the Mercury cycle.

The next book in the series is *The Great Wheel*, which discusses reincarnation in terms of the symbolism of the moon's monthly cycle. It is a commentary on William Butler Yeats' masterpiece *A Vision*.

The only other how-to books on magic which I would recommend are those of Franz Bardon, particularly his first book *Initiation into Hermetics*. This book is very much in the occidental tradition of magic and is more what the reader might expect of a book on magic – wands and pentacles and magic robes and circles and incantations and so forth. However, unlike most such books this one imparts a good grasp of the core concepts of magic – namely self-analysis and self-hypnosis. I would say that Bardon's books are better for dreamers and my books are better for stalkers. Magic is such a personal issue, however, that it's good to read different takes on the subject to create a praxis of one's own.

Unquestionably the best books on sexual magic are those of Mantak Chia, a Taoist master resident in the west. The idea is to refrain from orgasm and instead circulate the chi energy, the sub-orgasmic feeling, up your spine and around your body (or through both bodies during intercourse) instead of blowing it out your genitals. When the energy is circulating it opens doorways to higher states of consciousness. I've tried these techniques personally and was getting excellent results from them until my marriage broke up. At that point I let it slide, but I plan to resume the practice. The general theory behind chi energy, and good exercises which are not specifically sexual, are contained in Chia's introductory volume *Awaken Healing Energy Through the Tao*. There are two follow-up volumes, one for men: *Taoist Secrets of Love – Cultivating Male Sexual Energy*; and one for women: *Healing Love Through the Tao – Cultivating Female Sexual Energy*.

List of Books Cited Above:

*Especially recommended for the casual reader who doesn't intend to plow through the entire list.

Abelar, Taisha, *The Sorcerer's Crossing*, Arkana NYC 1992

Bardon, Franz, *Initiation into Hermetics*, Dieter Ruggeberg, Wuppertal Germany 1971

Bardon, Franz, *The Practice of Magical Evocation*, Dieter Ruggeberg, Wuppertal Germany 1970

Bardon, Franz, *The Key to the True Quabbalah*, Dieter Ruggeberg, Wuppertal Germany 1972

Brennan, Barbara, *Light Emerging,* Bantam NYC 1993

Castaneda, Carlos, *The Teachings of Don Juan – A Yaqui Way of Knowledge*, U. of California Press LA 1968

Castaneda, Carlos, *A Separate Reality*, Simon & Schuster NYC 1971

*Castaneda, Carlos, *Journey to Ixtlan*, Simon & Schuster NYC 1972

*Castaneda, Carlos, *Tales of Power*, Simon & Schuster NYC 1974

Castaneda, Carlos, *The Second Ring of Power*, Simon & Schuster NYC 1977

Castaneda, Carlos, *The Eagle's Gift*, Simon & Schuster NYC 1981

Castaneda, Carlos, *The Fire From Within*, Simon & Schuster NYC 1984

*Castaneda, Carlos, *The Power of Silence*, Simon & Schuster NYC 1987

Castaneda, Carlos, *The Art of Dreaming*, HarperCollins NYC 1993

What is Magic?

Castaneda, Carlos, *The Active Side of Infinity*, HarperCollins NYC 1998

Castaneda, Carlos, *Magical Passes*, HarperCollins NYC 1998

Chia, Mantak, *Awaken Healing Energy Through the Tao*, Aurora NYC 1983

Chia, Mantak, *Taoist Secrets of Love – Cultivating Male Sexual Energy*, Aurora NYC 1984

Chia, Mantak, *Healing Love Through the Tao – Cultivating Female Sexual Energy*, Aurora NYC 1986

Donner, Florinda, *Being-In-Dreaming*, HarperCollins NYC 1991

*Donner, Florinda, *The Witch's Dream*, Simon & Schuster NYC 1985

Gawain, Shakti, *Creative Visualization*, Bantam NYC 1982

Johnson, Robert, *Inner Work*, Harper & Row San Francisco 1986

LaBerge, Stephen, *Lucid Dreaming*, Ballantine NYC 1986

LaBerge, Stephen and Rheingold, Howard, *Exploring the World of Lucid Dreaming*, Ballantine NYC 1990

Makransky, Bob, *Magical Living*, Dear Brutus Press 2001, paperback at: http://www.amzn.com/1499279337; ebook at: www.smashwords.com/books/view/22860

Makransky, Bob, *Thought Forms*, Dear Brutus Press 2000, paperback at: http://www.amzn.com/1499267444; ebook at: www.smashwords.com/books/view/22859

Makransky, Bob, *The Great Wheel*, Dear Brutus Press 2013, paperback at: http://www.amzn.com/154416355X; ebook at: www.smashwords.com/books/view/306020

Monroe, Robert, *Journeys Out of the Body*, Anchor NYC 1971

Ophiel (Clarence Peach), *The Art and Practice of Astral Projection*, Weiser NYC 1961

Roberts, Jane, *Seth Speaks*, Bantam NYC 1972

Roberts, Jane, *The Nature of Personal Reality*, Bantam NYC 1980

Torres, Armando, *Encounters with the Nagual – Conversations with Carlos Castaneda*, First Light 2004

Glossary

Active imagination – a technique for consciously interacting with our thought forms

Cognition – making sense of what is perceived; the feeling that what is happening is familiar and important

Creative Visualization – a technique for imagining our desires coming true in the here and now

Customary moods and *concerns* – importance coverings: our thought forms' thought forms. They are feelings of self-pity conjured up by our constantly thinking thoughts of shame and glory

Desire lines – light fibers of desire, which are emitted from our navels and with which we reach out to bring ourselves the probable realities in which those desires are realized

Enlightenment – operating with our higher self rather than lower self

Higher self – our true feelings, intent; what we are really feeling in our inmost hearts

Importance – urgency, the feeling that something needs to be paid attention to (or ignored). It is importance which enables us to focus our awareness

Intent – higher self; impeccability; our innate sense of what is right and true, of who we are and what we must do; our purpose – the reason we were born in this lifetime

Karma – decisions made in other lifetimes and realities which inform and shape this present one

Light fibers – feelings, which is what the universe actually consists of. To psychic vision feelings appear as fibers of living light. In humans they emerge from the navel and form an egg-shaped aura around the body

Lower self – our self-pity (which includes our body). It is created by our thinking

Lucid dreaming – dreaming in which we are aware that we are dreaming

Magic – the intentional manipulation of luck by means of the deliberate cultivation of intuition

Planetary Hours – an ancient Chaldean system for choosing propitious times to act based upon which planet rules each hour of the day

Probable realities – parallel lives which branch off from this present life history whenever a decision is made

Recapitulation – a technique similar to past life regressions for reliving memories from this lifetime

Self-pity – the belief that we are special; and that there is a "me" to whom things are happening

Society – the set of conceptual thought forms (sometimes termed "memes") which are common to a particular milieu at a particular time

The Spirit – the magician's God. It is the source of light fibers, i.e. everything that exists is a manifestation of it. Unlike the Judeo-Christian-Islamic God it is utterly indifferent, so there is no point in worshipping it or praying to it. Nonetheless it is subject to our intent by means of unyielding determination and infinite patience.

Thought form – a thought (= *conceptual thought form*) or sensation (sight, sound, smell, taste, touch = *sensory thought form*). In this book the simple term "thought form" usually means conceptual thought form – a response / reaction learned from parents or society. Thought forms are analogous to homunculi in cognitive philosophy: sensory thought forms are analogous to qualia, and conceptual thought forms are analogous to agents, memes or schema control units.

BOOKS BY BOB MAKRANSKY:

Bob Makransky's **Introduction to Magic** Series:
"In this series, not only do we get an author who knows his subject inside out, but also a directness of approach often not seen in works of this kind. Not for Makransky the wishy-washy approach that attempts to soothe and reassure the reader with false promises of magical success - something about which many customer complaints arise on the Amazon website - but, rather, an honest and uncompromising study of what Magic really entails. – James Lynn Page (author of *Celtic Magic*, *Everyday Tarot* and *The Christ Enigma*)

What is Magic?, the introductory book on witchcraft, can be sampled and purchased at:
Paperback $19.95: **http://www.amzn.com/1499279418**
ebook $9.95: **www.smashwords.com/books/view/132491**
Kindle edition: **www.amzn.com/B0079K8X9O**

Magical Living, about paganism, can be sampled and purchased at:
Paperback $16.95: **http://www.amzn.com/1499279337**
ebook $9.95: **www.smashwords.com/books/view/22860**
Kindle edition: **www.amzn.com/B0041843ZU**

Thought Forms, about cognitive psychology and the Mercury cycle, can be sampled and purchased at:
Paperback $24.95: **http://www.amzn.com/1499267444**
ebook $9.95: **www.smashwords.com/books/view/22859**
Kindle edition: **www.amzn.com/B00439H1F6**

The Great Wheel, about reincarnation and the lunar cycle, is available for $24.95 from:
http://www.amzn.com/154416355X
ebook $9.95: **www.smashwords.com/books/view/306020**
Kindle edition: **www.amzn.com/B00CD958PS**

Volume II of Bob's Introduction to Magic series:

Magical Living

Winner of the Reader Views Reviewer's Choice Award and the Sacramento Publishers' Association awards for Best Nonfiction and Best Spiritual book; Mind-Body-Spirit category finalist in the National Indie Excellence Awards and the USA Book News Best Books Awards; *Magical Living* is a collection of essays which give detailed, how-to instructions on channeling spirit guides, communicating with plants and nature spirits, developing your psychic vision; together with inspirational essays on managing love relationships, handling oppressive people, and dealing with hurt.

"I love this little book! ... Carry this book with you, read and reread the essays, and connect with joy." – Kathryn Lanier, *InnerChange* magazine

"He writes beautifully, clearly, elegantly ... he is incapable of an unoriginal thought." – Joseph Polansky, *Diamond Fire* magazine

"I could not get enough! I actually read some of the essays 2 to 3 times and discovered new insights each time. ... 'Magical Living' by Bob Makransky is an easy to read little book with a lot of surprises. A great book to revisit more than once!" – Susan Violante, *Reader Views*

Magical Living paperback - $16.95 at:
http://www.amzn.com/1499279337
Magical Living ebook - $9.95 at:
www.smashwords.com/books/view/22860
Kindle edition: **www.amzn.com/B0041843ZU**

Volume III of Bob's Introduction to Magic series

Thought Forms

Astronomical and astrological explanations of Mercury's synodic cycle – its cycle of phases as it circles the sun, with tables 1900-2050.

Complete delineations for Superior and Inferior Conjunction, Greatest Eastern and Western Elongation, Stationary Retrograde and Direct, and their intervening phases in the natal, progressed, and transiting horoscopes.

Explanation of the astrological / magical view of mind (the theory of Thought Forms): what consciousness is, how it arose, and whither it is going.

Basic course in white magic with detailed instructions on: How to Channel and Banish Thought Forms; Creative Visualization; How to banish the Black Magicians in everyday life; How to Cast out Demons; How to use Tree Spirits.

"Bob Makransky is a knowledgeable, purposeful and entertaining writer." – Paul F. Newman, *The International Astrologer* magazine

"Steady Diamond Fire *readers are well acquainted with the genius of Bob Makransky. Highly recommendable."* – Joseph Polansky, *Diamond Fire* magazine

"Readers have become familiar with [Makransky's] fresh insights into different facets of astrology. In this book Thought Forms *he is especially provocative and I strongly recommend its purchase and study."* – Ken Gillman, *Considerations* magazine

"I will fully agree with the statement that 'You've never read a book like this before!' The material is fresh and woven very skillfully to conclusion. I look forward to his next installment of the trilogy." – Marion MacMillan, *SHAPE*

Thought Forms Paperback $24.95 from:
http://www.amzn.com/1499267444
Thought Forms ebook $9.95 can be sampled and purchased at: www.smashwords.com/books/view/22859
Kindle edition: https://www.amzn.com/B00439H1F6

* * * * * * *

Volume IV of Bob's Introduction to Magic series:

The Great Wheel

"On the afternoon of October 24th, 1917, four days after my marriage, my wife surprised me by attempting automatic writing. What came in disjointed sentences, in almost illegible writing, was so exciting, sometimes so profound, that I ... offered to spend what remained of life explaining and piecing together those scattered sentences."
– William Butler Yeats

It is often said in spiritual literature that time and space are an illusion, *maya*, *samsara*. But what exactly does this mean? And what implications does it have for how you should live your everyday life? *The Great Wheel* is an explanation of the System of birth, death, and rebirth which Nobel laureate William Butler Yeats' described in his masterpiece, *A Vision*.

Starting out with a discussion of how you can connect with your true purpose in this life – the reason why you incarnated on the earth at this time – *The Great Wheel* describes simple techniques you can use (such as past life regressions, probable reality progressions, and recapitulation of present life memories) to glimpse different facets of your *Daimon* (your oversoul; the totality of who you are), in order to understand clearly how you got to where you are at right now. To live your true life's purpose rather than drift along helplessly, it is necessary to see how your present life situation is the end result of decisions which you, yourself, made in other lifetimes and realities.

An in-depth discussion of twenty-eight personality types (depending upon where you were born in the moon's monthly cycle of phases) illuminates your individual true purpose in incarnating in this life, and helps you to understand where you belong and where you are going. *The Great Wheel* concludes with a fascinating explanation of what reality is all about: Mind and Memory, Waking and Dreaming, Change, Familiarity, and the Akashic Records.

"This new work in Bob Makransky's excellent and thought provoking 'Introduction to Magic' series ... is a fascinating and illuminating take on the meaning of the Moon. It's truly a Moon book unlike any other and is guaranteed to alter your perception of yourself and the world." – Paul F. Newman, author *LUNA: The Astrological Moon*

"*This is not the kind of book you just read and it's finished. It's really a work book. You have to practice the exercises he gives. You have to apply the lunar phases to your own chart and to others. Not beach reading material. Be prepared to be educated and also shocked!*" - Joseph Polansky, *Diamond Fire* magazine

"*It is difficult to change thought patterns to find a new path, and that is the primary reason I read* The Great Wheel *and encourage others to read it. It is very deep, thorough and forces one to step back and start looking at the big picture. What picture of your life is in need of help? What aspect of your personality could use some help? This book has the tools to help you*". - Peggy Mathias, *Psychic-Magic* magazine

The Great Wheel
$24.95 from **http://www.amzn.com/154416355X**
ebook $9.95 can be sampled and purchased at:
www.smashwords.com/books/view/306020
Kindle edition: **http://www.amzn.com/B00CD958PS**

Intermediate Level Astrology Textbooks:

Topics in Astrology

A delightful cornucopia of over three dozen essays on a wide variety of astrological topics ranging from practical, hands-on advice to technical issues to humor and satire. *Topics in Astrology* is chock-full of original tips and guidelines for experienced practitioners (it may be a bit advanced for beginners, but even they will find parts of the book fascinating).

Partial Contents:

The natal horoscopes of Philadelphia hippie guru-cum-murderer Ira Einhorn and polygamist Mormon guru-cum-murderer Ervil LeBaron are thoroughly analyzed; as is the abortive romance between Nobel laureate William Butler Yeats and the unattainable beauty Maud Gonne. Exhaustive, in-depth discussions of how transits, primary directions, and secondary progressions work are illustrated with scores of examples taken from the horoscopes of notables. How to use astrolocality (employing astrology to find favorable and avoid unfavorable places to live or visit) is described in detail. The traditional rules of horary astrology are examined and evaluated in the cases of the *Titanic* disaster and the Nixon resignation. The rules of electional astrology are illustrated in a chapter on how to pick winning lottery tickets. The validity of eclipses and comets is examined; and technical issues such as how house systems are constructed are discussed in depth. Oh yes – Bob pokes fun at astrology too, with convincing analyses of the natal horoscopes (including predictions which came true!) for a couple of fictional characters.

"The sheer scope of the work is mind boggling. Bob Makransky has thought deeply and cogently on the subject and it shows. He shows aspects of Astrology that are outside the current mainstream. A very recommendable book for the serious astrological student." – Joseph Polansky, *Diamond Fire* magazine

"*Makransky expounds on numerous subjects of interest to astrologers in his anthology of published articles,* Topics in Astrology. *Makransky's plainspoken writing style is direct, full of absolutes, and thought-provoking. Beginners will enjoy and frequently refer to many of the articles. With his wide-ranging interests, Makransky offers something for everyone"* – Chris Lorenz, Dell Horoscope magazine

Topics in Astrology 312 pages paperback $22.95
order from: **http://www.amzn.com/1519765878**
Kindle edition $9.99 from:
http://www.amazon.com/dp/B019NSBP4Y

* * * * * * *

Planetary Strength
– a commentary on Morinus

An essential contribution to natal horoscope interpretation. Taking as its point of departure *Astrologia Gallica* by Jean Baptiste Morin de Villefranche (1583 – 1656), *Planetary Strength* explains the differences between the strengths conferred upon planets by virtue of their sign placements (celestial state); house placements (terrestrial state); and aspects (aspectual state). A detailed system of keywords is augmented by insightful "cookbook" interpretations for each and every planetary combination. The depth and quality of the analysis – as well as the hundreds of practical examples and tips – make *Planetary Strength* an essential reference work which both neophyte and experienced practitioners will consult every time they read a horoscope.

"The book is beautifully written. With Makransky, whether you agree or disagree is not the issue - you will always get a good read. It is clear. He has done his homework. He makes the genius of Morinus accessible to English speakers. He shows us how to 'think astrologically'." – Joseph Polansky, *Diamond Fire* magazine

"What's fascinating about Planetary Strength *is that the author is using his own prose to describe the planets'*

conditions. In the introduction, he advises readers to study Morinus, but clearly Makransky's efforts are the better source. ... Try them in practice and compare these interpretations to what you might otherwise think about a planet. It may just sharpen your ability to make accurate statements about character, a person's history, and even to make predictions. And what more do you ask of astrology?" – Chris Lorenz, *Dell Horoscope* magazine

"This is certainly an interesting addition to reading and interpreting the translations of Morinus' original work. It is detailed and considered, and the author's knowledge and experience are evident throughout." – Helen Stokes, *AA Journal*

"Presenting a mixture of discussion, detailed cookbook offerings and chart examples as well as keywords and tables, this fascinating book also addresses the fixed stars. ... This fascinating book assumes a fair knowledge of astrology as well as some experience in preparing charts." – Margaret Gray, *ISAR*

"This is a book that every beginner as well as advanced student of astrology would do well to possess. The author is extremely perceptive in his descriptions of the planets in their various strength and weaknesses ... this book would be a helpful aid to the researcher, as it would point him in the right direction." – Wanda Sellar, *Correlation*

Planetary Strength 130 pages paperback £11.99
from:
http://www.wessexastrologer.com/product/waps001/

Planetary Combination

Planetary Combination picks up where *Planetary Strength* left off, explaining how the planetary influences combine in aspects and configurations to paint a picture of a person and his or her life. Descriptions of planetary configurations such as Grand Trines, Grand Squares, T-Crosses, Wedges, Fans, Rectangles, Kites, and Trapezoids provide overall schematics of people's psychological dynamics. Then, detailed interpretations for the conjunctions, sextiles/trines, squares, oppositions, parallels/contraparallels, and Mutual Receptions between the individual planets enable the practitioner to see clearly how these dynamics work out in a particular horoscope. An illuminating chapter on planetary conjunctions with the moon's nodes reveals the underlying karmic influences at work. An indispensable reference you'll consult every time you read a chart.

"While this book is nominally a series of explanations about aspects between the traditional planets, the degree of character description for each planetary pair is extraordinarily precise. An entire personality is captured within these aspects. In the same way that the author provides highly detailed character sketches for each planetary duo, he gives the same attention to configurations. In addition to the most common shapes, he also provides several pages on shapes that are not found in any other astrology text. An unusually terse and bold reference, Planetary Combination *transcends psychological mumbo-jumbo to give you the bare-naked reality of the adult Western psyche."* – Chris Lorenz, *Dell Horoscope magazine.*

"Planetary Combination is an excellent and comprehensive summary of all the relevant chart factors. ... One has to search hard to find such material! But this is all presented, as is all of Makransky's work, with vigour, wisdom and accessibility. Planetary Combination *fills a gap in the current state of astrological literature. It manages to retain both a sense of firm tradition whilst feeling utterly new and fresh."* –

James Lynn Page, author of *Everyday Tarot*, *Celtic Magic*, *The Christ Enigma* and *The New Positive Thinking*.

"This is one of the best books on aspects out there. He not only deals with aspects themselves, but goes deep into chart morphology. A student would have to read many books from many authors to get the information that is given here. As always with Bob Makransky's work, the book is interesting and well written, not for a beginner or casual reader, but fascinating nevertheless - especially for a serious student." – Joseph Polansky, *Diamond Fire* magazine

"You are entering a world of verbal complexity and conceptual subtlety. There is plenty that you have not seen anywhere else. You may find Makransky's approach to astrology brilliantly unconventional or just plain weird. I find little romance and no sentiment in Makransky's work.

"There is much to be gained from Makransky's presentation of life. I have clients and students for whom his set of attitudes is not uncommon and his prescriptions can be helpful. You may profit from Makransky's insightfulness and wisdom without having to buy into his world view: engaging in dialogue with his writing can clarify your own perspectives and stimulate your interpretative thinking into new directions.

"Think of studying this material like going to a 'blockbuster' art show and spending a fine afternoon with the art and vision of a Goya or a Van Gogh or an Escher, artists whose vision you may not share but whose perspectives you can learn from. I applaud Bob Makransky and his publisher Margaret Cahill at Wessex Astrologer for having produced a work of originality and complexity and befuddlement, astonishment and irritation and inspiration." – Joseph Crane, Astrology Institute

Planetary Combination 232 pages paperback £17.50 from:
http://www.wessexastrologer.com/product/wapc001/

Planetary Hours

The Planetary Hours are an ancient astrological system for selecting favorable times to act (and avoiding unfavorable times), by assigning planetary rulers to the twenty-four hours of the day. This book has easy-to-follow instructions for finding your birthday and birth hour rulers, and clearly explains how these determine your personality and your luck. A chapter on electional astrology explains how to use the Planetary Hours to find lucky times to act (to ask for money; to ask someone on a date or to marry; to go on a journey; to begin a new business). The chapter on How to Cast Spells gives the low-down on how to make magical spells (and prayers) *really* work, using simple astrological techniques. The use of the Firdaria, an ancient astrological prediction system which indicates positive and negative periods during a lifetime, is illustrated with a detailed analysis of events in the life of Theodore Roosevelt. Complete Tables of Planetary Hours at the end of the book allow you to find favorable times to initiate activities for any day of the year, and for anywhere on earth from the Equator to 58° North and South latitudes.

"Bob Makransky ... describes Planetary Hours (PH) as the 'astrology of luck' and a method of finding empowering life moments for the proper exercise of freewill – to be yourself and not an enslaved cog of convention – Makransky explains in this admirably lucid guide book. As an introduction, this book is highly accessible." – AA Journal

"Bob Makransky has written the definitive book on Planetary Hours. It's the best book on the subject out there. It will be read and studied by future generations of astrologers. It's not just something that you read and discard. You want it in your bookshelf to refer to again and again." – Joseph Polansky, *Diamond Fire* magazine

Planetary Hours 118 pages paperback £11.00
from:
http://www.wessexastrologer.com/product/waph001/

www.ingramcontent.com/pod-product-compliance
Lightning Source LLC
Chambersburg PA
CBHW050635300426
44112CB00012B/1807